# Our Untold Stories

# Our Untold Stories

## EXTRAORDINARY TALES FROM NEW ZEALAND'S PAST

## TOM CLARKE

BATEMAN BOOKS

Text © Tom Clarke, 2023
Typographical design © David Bateman Ltd, 2023
Published in 2023 by David Bateman Ltd
2/5 Workspace Drive, Hobsonville, Auckland 0618, New Zealand
www.batemanbooks.co.nz

ISBN 978-1-77689-068-2

Cover and book design: Cheryl Smith
All featured images are copyright their respective titleholders.

Front cover images: Auckland Island rescue raft: Collection of the Southland Museum and Art Gallery, Accession Number: 83.3387; Pounamu: Julia Bradshaw, Canterbury Museum; Waco aircraft: Walsh Memorial Library, The Museum of Transport & Technology (MOTAT); Sparrow: Dr Phil Battley, Asst Professor in Zoology, School of Natural Sciences, Massey University, Palmerston North.
Back cover images: Painting of Te Heuheu Tūkino II by George French Angas: Wikimedia Commons; Airship: Airship Heritage Trust, UK, www.airshiponline.com; State house: Ref: APG-0448-1/2-G, Alexander Turnbull Library, Wellington, New Zealand.

Printed in China through Colorcraft Ltd, Hong Kong

# CONTENTS

**Firsts**

**Human Nature**

**Religion**

**Scoundrels, Rascals and Shysters**

# INTRODUCTION

This book had its beginnings in 1983 when I began compiling my *Today in History New Zealand* — a daily catalogue of the news and events that have shaped New Zealand, beginning with the very first recorded European sighting made by Abel Janszoon Tasman on 13 December 1642.

When I started compiling that, there was no comprehensive daily diary of New Zealand events and as far as I am aware, there still isn't, apart from my own chronicle of events. As happens today, many newspapers at the time did run 'Today in History' features, which were provided by overseas news agencies such as the Australian Associated Press (AAP). By virtue of their source, the events they covered were almost exclusively overseas events, except where New Zealand events had been of such magnitude or importance that they made the pages of major overseas newspapers.

*Today in History New Zealand* was a service provided to radio stations around the country for their on-air staff to drop into their programmes. National Radio, and specifically the afternoon host, Wayne Mowat, was a long-time customer and user of the material.

Over the intervening 40 years of ongoing research, *Today in History New Zealand* has grown into the most comprehensive record of newsworthy or noteworthy events that have occurred in this country, with some 4000 recorded events spread over all 365 days of the year, plus Leap Day.

The original sources for this information have been wide ranging from books and newspapers, through family anecdotes and educational theses, to magazines and websites.

It also resulted in the discovery of many fascinating, forgotten stories of early New Zealand, a collection of which makes up the contents of this book — stories about human tragedies, about bravery and daring endeavours, stories that reflect the enormous changes that have occurred in the thinking, opinions, beliefs and attitudes of New Zealanders over the years, and stories that are just sheer entertainment to read today.

I am indebted to many people for this book. Thanks to Wendy Hill and Mike Edgar for their proofreading and critical analysis of the copy, to my author-daughter Serena Clarke for her creative input, and to my friend and lawyer Barry Hopkins for his guidance on legal issues of the past. Thanks also to Wendy and Serena for their encouragement and support.

My grateful thanks also to Adrian Kinnaird, Senior Editor, Bateman Books, and to Louise Russell, Publisher at Bateman Books, for their support of this project.

And finally, if you have further information about any of the stories in this book, or if you have any fascinating stories from the past that we should know about, please feel free to email me at kiwitombo@gmail.com

Tom Clarke
Taupō

# All at Sea

# 1846

# FIRST STEAMSHIP TO VISIT NEW ZEALAND JOINS LAND WAR

The first steamship to visit New Zealand, the Royal Navy Driver-class wooden sloop, HMS *Driver* — which was also the first steamship to circumnavigate the globe — arrived in Auckland on 20 January 1846.

Driver-class sloops were a class of warship that combined sail and steam. They had two or three masts for sails along with steam-powered paddles, and a single gun-deck that carried up to eighteen guns. The Royal Navy ordered 21 of the ships, but only six were built.

HMS *Driver* had two masts, weighed in at 1058 tons, and had a coal-fired two-cylinder steam engine producing about 280 hp. It had been designed by controversial Royal Naval architect, Sir William Symonds, and was built at the Portsmouth Dockyard in southern England with its steam engine made by Seaward & Capel of Limehouse, Woolwich. It was launched on 24 December 1840, and commissioned on 5 November 1841, at a total cost of £39,700.

It was armed with six large guns — four 42-pounder guns and

two 68-pounder guns — and had a complement of 175 officers and crew.

The ship ran aground twice while undergoing trials off Yorkshire and had to enter dry dock for repairs, after which, in March 1842, it sailed for the East Indies and China, despite concerns in some quarters within the Navy about the adequacy of the ship's boilers for such a long and important deployment.

*Driver* joined the East India Station of the Royal Navy in June 1842 and was involved in suppressing piracy in the seas around the East Indies until 1845 when it was ordered to proceed to New Zealand to support British military units here. In September it was in Hong Kong, China where the boilers were inspected and found to be suspect, but because of the deteriorating military situation in New Zealand it was felt the ship had to proceed, nonetheless.

It left Hong Kong, China for New Zealand on 27 September, but between Taiwan, China and the Philippines, en route to Guam in early October, it ran into a severe hurricane which blew out its sails and for twelve hours left the ship at the mercy of the wind and sea. Bulwarks, railings, several deck boats and the cookhouse were swept away.

On 8 October, after the storm abated, *Driver* began steaming towards Singapore for repairs when a leak was discovered in one of the boilers, which had to be shut down. This was followed by a rush of boiling water into the engine room from the other boiler. The ship's chief engineer, at some risk to his own safety, managed to put out the fire in the boiler and open a safety valve, averting the risk of more damage.

But with its main sails blown out and its boilers out of action and requiring at least four days for repairs to be made, the ship was helpless until enough temporary sail could be set to provide some way and therefore some control.

On 14 October, with temporary repairs made at sea, one boiler was fired up and *Driver* was heading for Singapore under paddle-power when another leak was discovered in the boiler, a situation made worse by the fact that the boiler was being run at full capacity. Despite the risks involved it was able to struggle on and — perhaps as a tribute to the manufacturer of the machinery — *Driver* made the voyage to Singapore at an average seven knots, a fast pace considering the mechanical drawbacks it was operating under.

Full repairs were made to the ship's structure and machinery in Singapore, and it departed for New Zealand on 6 November 1845.

In December it arrived at Fremantle, Western Australia, where it caused consternation among the locals who, on seeing a ship approaching and billowing clouds of smoke, thought it was a vessel on fire until it got close enough to shore for them to realise what it was.

By January HMS *Driver* was in Sydney to replenish its dwindling fuel supply with 500 tons of coal in preparation for the voyage across the Tasman and its activities around our coast.

But there were insufficient coal stocks available in Sydney for the ship's needs, and it was deemed too risky for it to sail to Newcastle to collect supplies because of its size and draught, so a fleet of smaller boats was organised to bring coal to Sydney for its bunkers.

HMS *Driver* left Sydney on 15 January 1846, and arrived in Auckland

*The steam paddle sloop HMS* Driver *enters Port Jackson (Sydney) on its historic voyage, January 1846, en route to New Zealand and to becoming the first steam vessel to circumnavigate the globe. Watercolour, artist unknown.*
Mitchell Library, Sydney

on 20 January, to become the first engine-powered vessel seen in New Zealand waters.

Reports at the time said the ship was carrying £5000 worth of gold and £5000 worth of silver, funding for the colonial government in New Zealand. It was followed by the barque *Celia* which was carrying 1500 tons of coal from Australia to keep the ship supplied while operating here.

HMS *Driver* arrived as the Northern War was coming to an end, and there is no record of it being involved in that conflict despite the large number of Royal Navy and British ships that were moving men and equipment to and from the Bay of Islands. But later it did become involved in the land wars in Wellington.

The Northern War had begun on 11 March 1845, when Hōne Heke and Te Ruki Kawiti led an attack on the settlement of Kororāreka which led to the township being abandoned two days later, with civilians and military boarding a fleet of five ships and fleeing to Auckland while their town burnt to the ground. The fleet included the Royal Navy Frigate HMS *Hazard*, the US warship *St Louis*, the British whaling ship *Matilda*, Bishop Selwyn's schooner *Flying Fish* and the government brig *Victoria*.

Fighting in the north dragged on with much loss of life on both sides until British forces launched an attack against Heke and Kawiti's Ruapekapeka pā on 10 January 1846, which, after a determined defence by the pā's 500 defenders, fell the following day, bringing the ten-month-old Northern War to an end.

With an uneasy peace in Northland, Governor George Grey was able to withdraw troops from there and reposition them in Wellington where there was increasing unease between Māori and Pākehā over land issues.

With Governor Grey aboard, HMS *Driver*, along with the Royal Navy frigates *Castor* and *Calliope* and the brigs *Victoria*, *Bark* and *Slains Castle*, left Auckland on 3 February bound for Wellington. The fleet also transported almost 600 soldiers as reinforcements for the 200 troops already stationed there.

The arrival of the fleet caused quite a stir in Wellington, not only because of the number of soldiers it brought but also the presence of HMS *Driver* as the first steamship to enter Port Nicholson.

The spectacle of *Driver* enthralled Wellingtonians and according to reports at the time, astounded local Māori who gathered to watch the strange ship which they saw sailing with 'fire inside and which fought easily and quickly against wind and tide'. In the Hutt Valley, skirmishes had occurred between Māori and European settlers over land seizures. This came to a head on 3 March 1846, with an attack on British troops stationed at Boulcott's farm which was located north-east of the present-day Hutt Valley CBD. The land was farmed by Almon Boulcott who came to New Zealand in 1842, but his presence was opposed by local Māori, Ngāti Hāua-te-rangi. Tensions boiled over when two Lower Hutt settlers, Andrew Gillespie and his thirteen-year-old son, were attacked and killed with tomahawks on 2 April. It was thought the attackers had sought shelter at the Taupō pā of the influential chief Te Rauparaha near present-day Plimmerton beach. It was widely believed that Te Rauparaha, who had declared himself neutral, was supporting and sheltering the attackers, a view that gained strength after letters were captured that showed he was playing a secret double game.

Governor Grey's view was that Te Rauparaha could not be trusted and should be arrested and charged with supplying weapons to the attackers, and HMS *Driver* was closely involved in an action which became a decisive factor in his capture.

With rumours of a pending attack on Wellington, Grey went aboard *Driver* to sail to Plimmerton to visit Te Rauparaha at the pā. After that meeting Grey left on *Driver*, but just before dawn on 22 July 1846, the ship returned to Taupō pā and in a secret raid, a group of sailors from *Driver* entered the pā and arrested the chief on a charge of treason.

Te Rauparaha was held on HMS *Calliope*, reportedly more as a guest than as a prisoner, until he was released ten months later when tempers had cooled, and he went to live in Auckland. He returned to the area in 1848 and lived at Ōtaki until his death on 27 November 1849.

HMS *Driver* returned to Auckland after the Taupō pā action and later sailed to the Bay of Islands. For the next twelve months it was active around the New Zealand coastline and apparently made one or two voyages to Sydney and back. In January 1847 it was once again dispatched from Auckland to Northland with a detachment of soldiers to 'quell an insurrection' by Hōne Heke.

On 27 January 1847, it left New Zealand to return to England via Cape Horn, with another Royal Navy steam sloop — HMS *Inflexible* — taking its place in New Zealand.

*Driver* stopped in Argentina to restock its coal and water supplies and arrived back at Portsmouth on 14 May, completing the first global circumnavigation by a steamship, a voyage that had actually taken five years and covered a total of 75,696 miles (121,820 km).

In fact, most of the voyage was made under sail because of the difficulty of obtaining coal supplies for the boilers in most parts of the world at that time.

HMS *Driver* continued in active service for the next fourteen years in North America, the Mediterranean, the Pacific and in the Baltic during the Crimean War. Its service ended when it was wrecked on Mayaguana Island in the Bahamas on a voyage from Bermuda to Jamaica on 3 August 1861.

# 1867

# DESPERATE BID FOR HELP FAILS

The dramatic story of the wreck of the *General Grant* on the rugged cliffs of Auckland Island, late at night on 13 May 1866, is well known and well documented.

What isn't so well known is the heroic efforts of the desperate survivors to reach civilisation and organise a rescue, a sad and inspiring tale of human courage and enterprise in the face of appalling odds.

The *General Grant* was a three-masted, timber-hulled barque of about 1100 tons. Built in the Bath shipyard of R. Morse & Sons in Maine in the United States it was launched into the Kennebec River in February 1864. The ship was named after the famous Civil War general and future US president, Ulysses S. Grant and was one of a number built by the company named after Civil War leaders.

It was a large vessel built for hard work and heavy seas, being nearly 55 metres long and with a beam of 10.5 metres and was owned by the American company, Boyes, Richardson & Co.

It sailed from the Kennebec River to Boston where it took on its first cargo, which was a consignment of stagecoaches bound for San Francisco and the Californian Pioneer Stage Company.

The *General Grant* left Boston on 10 March 1864, on its maiden 19,000-mile voyage around Cape Horn to San Francisco, with Albion P. Alexander as its captain.

(As an interesting aside, one of those stagecoaches aboard was reputedly driven in Wyoming by Martha Jane Cannary, better known as Calamity Jane, and later became part of the William Cody (Buffalo Bill) Wild West show in the US and Europe. That coach is now in the Buffalo Bill Historic Museum in Cody, Wyoming.)

Its next voyage was to Singapore and India, and it left San Francisco on 7 November 1864, arriving in Calcutta in March 1865. That was followed by a trip back to Boston via the Cape of Good Hope where it arrived in late September, having completed a circumnavigation of the globe. At Boston the ship was resurveyed, and a new captain took command, William H. Loughlin, who was also a part-owner of the vessel.

In November 1865 the *General Grant* departed Boston for Melbourne via the Cape of Good Hope, arriving off Port Phillip Head at the entrance to Melbourne in February 1866.

On 4 May the ship left Melbourne on its ill-fated voyage to London via Cape Horn. It was laden with a mixed cargo that included 2057 bales of wool, animal skins, woollens, leather, along with 2576 ounces of gold and nine tons of zinc spelter ballast. There was a crew of 25 and a full complement of 58 passengers aboard, including six women and 20 children and a number of goldminers who were returning to England — perhaps with their spoils — after success on the Australian goldfields. Mindful of its cargo, the owners took out insurance of £165,000 for the voyage.

From Australia to England is about 23,700 km and the *General Grant* was expected to take about 100 days to complete the trip. Leaving Melbourne's Hobson Bay, it headed south to catch the clipper ship route which provided sailing ships with the fastest journey to Europe from Australia and New Zealand. The route took in the 'Roaring Forties' and the 'Furious Fifties', west to east trade winds, and the east-bound Antarctic Circumpolar Current which carried sailing ships along at a fast pace. There was, however, significant risk from extreme winds, huge seas, icebergs, isolated islands and dangerous land formations like Cape Horn at the foot of South America.

They tended to travel as far south as possible where the westerly winds were strongest and drove ships fastest, but where the risks were greatest.

Compounding the dangers was the fact that navigation charts of the time could be wildly inaccurate. In 1868, for instance, it was found that the 1851 chart commonly in use positioned the Auckland Islands 56 kilometres south of where they actually were.

The *General Grant* was making good progress in fair conditions. It had had fine weather with light westerly winds as it headed east towards South America.

Captain Loughlin took a sextant reading at eight o'clock in the morning of 11 May, but after that the weather closed in with a heavy fog making it impossible to make any further observations. On Sunday, 13 May, he ordered a sharp lookout for land, and at about 10.30 that night land was sighted off the port bow. That was Disappointment Island, part of the Auckland Island archipelago, north-west of the main island.

All hands were called on deck and the order given to 'square away the yard', that is to set the sails directly before the wind to increase speed and manoeuvrability. This was done, and the ship carried on. Shortly after land was sighted again, this time on the starboard bow.

At the same time, the wind began to drop and a few minutes later it became dead calm, but the south-west swell and current continued to carry the ship along. The *General Grant* had become totally unmanageable and was in a very perilous position.

Later a survivor described their position:

> The captain did all in his power, with every flaw of wind from the flapping sails, but his attempts were useless. The yards were hauled in every possible direction that might enable the getting his ship off the shore, but all to no purpose, as the heavy S. W. swell was constantly setting her nearer and nearer the fatal rocks.

As midnight passed the ship's fate was sealed: the strong current carried the ship northwards along the Auckland Island west coast until it hit the rocky cliffs of the island bow-on, which broke off the fore-boom stay and caused it to turn through 180 degrees. It continued backwards for about 500 metres until it hit rocks under the water, smashing the rudder and causing severe injuries to the seaman on the helm. The current then carried the helpless ship 90 metres into a deep cavity in the cliffs where chaos ensued.

In the darkness the rising tide and deep swell drove the masts into the roof of the cavern, smashing rocks down onto the ship. As the tide and swell, along with sharply increasing winds, pushed the stricken ship further into the dark cavern, the masts were broken off or driven through the bottom of the hull and the ship sank lower in the water.

Crewmen lit lanterns to provide some light, and they and the passengers — some only in their night attire — sought shelter from the falling rocks and rigging and the bitterly cold wind in the aft part of the ship as they waited for daylight so they could launch the lifeboats.

The *General Grant* carried three lifeboats — two quarterboats of about 7 metres each hanging from davits, and a 9-metre longboat. They managed to get some food aboard the boats, and one was lowered over the stern with three crewmen. They rowed out of the cavern in search of a landing site but found nothing suitable. A second quarterboat was launched with the chief officer, three crewmen and one passenger aboard, and as the *General Grant* sank the longboat on the quarterdeck floated free with about 40 passengers aboard but was swamped after getting clear of the wreck. Three of the passengers aboard managed to swim to the nearby quarterboat, which meant that from the original complement of 83, only fifteen had survived the sinking — nine crewmen and six passengers, including one woman, Mrs Mary Ann Jewell, the wife of Able-Bodied Seaman Joseph Jewell, who also survived.

Mrs Jewell's position aboard the *General Grant* is a little confusing. She was listed as a stewardess and had signed articles of employment for the voyage, but she did not act as a stewardess and in fact she had paid for her passage. It seems this was so she could join her husband on the voyage.

Captain Loughlin, in traditional maritime custom, went down with his ship. Survivors reported that they could see him and another person standing on the ship, waving a handkerchief just as it went under the water. They were not seen again.

Those in the quarterboat still inside the cavern spent some time searching for any further survivors, but they found no one alive. They were facing increasing danger from the high seas and wind, which forced them to abandon the search.

The survivors in the two boats were then faced with another dilemma — there was no shoreline in the area, just perpendicular cliffs some 120 metres high, meaning there was no possibility of them getting ashore. They decided to head for Disappointment Island about 10 kilometres to the west, and that proved to be a difficult task as they battled against high seas and strong winds in the open boats.

They had to keep bailing to keep the open boats afloat, and after struggling all day they finally reached the relative shelter of a large rocky islet just off Disappointment Island at nightfall, where they spent a wet and cold night having to constantly row to prevent the boats being blown out to sea. They had no water but were able to open some tins of bouilli (meat and vegetables) they had salvaged from the *General Grant*.

At daylight on 15 May, they attempted to row north-east towards the northern tip of Auckland Island, but the wind and current were too strong, so they turned back and headed for Disappointment Island where they were finally able to land. But in doing so, the boat that was carrying the meagre supplies they had managed to save from the *General Grant* overturned in the surf. They were only able to save nine tins of bouilli and three pieces of pork. But they were able to save the boat and to find fresh water on the island.

By mid-morning the wind had died away and the seas were dead calm, so the fifteen survivors returned to the boats and headed for Auckland Island, this time reaching North Harbour on the main island where they again spent a cold night without shelter. The next day they continued around the northern shores of the island, finally reaching Port Ross where they spent the next night sheltering among the ruins of Enderby settlement, the remains of a failed attempt to settle the island made by whaler Samuel Enderby that had been abandoned fifteen years earlier, in 1851.

They managed to get the last match they had in their possession to strike and start a fire, which they maintained during the next eighteen months. They were able to boil water in empty bouilli tins and cook some birds they had caught on Disappointment Island and some limpets they gathered on the shore of Port Ross. It was their first real meal in three days, and as one of the survivors wrote, 'never did sumptuous repast taste better to a king than this frugal meal to us'. The survivors then settled to the task of exploring the island in search of proper shelter and locating food, knowing that goats, rabbits and pigs had been left on the island to provide food for shipwreck survivors. They believed too that clothing and provisions had been stored in a depot. The need for shelter was paramount — many of the survivors were without shoes and socks, and most didn't have coats or hats to help keep them warm in the bitterly cold and wet climate. In their searches they located several derelict huts which they were able to patch up enough to provide rudimentary shelter. They were also able to find an old oven, some old canvas, some

*Victorian couple Joseph and Mary Ann Jewell, survivors of the General Grant wreck photographed in Melbourne in 1868. They are both wearing the sealskin garments that Mary Ann and James Teer, a miner, fashioned for the survivors, using needles carved from albatross bone with a penknife. The Jewells reportedly lost the fortune they had amassed in the Victorian goldfields in the disaster, but they found a profitable use for Mary Ann's unique clothes. She is said to have earned as much as £600 delivering lectures about the ordeal while dressed in her sealskin outfit.*

Photograph by Charles Hewitt, Melbourne, 1868. Gift of E. Webber, 1955. Ref: GH003129/5, Te Papa Tongarewa Museum of New Zealand

galvanised iron, a spade and a few other bits and pieces from the earlier settlements that would help them survive. As time went on, they were able to clothe themselves using sealskins.

They killed seals for food and shellfish were prolific, but most of the castaways suffered severe dysentery as a result, the debilitating illness making their struggles for survival even more difficult in the frigid winter conditions of sleet, snow and bitterly cold wind.

The onset of winter also meant that the whale- and seal-hunting season was over, seriously reducing the possibility of ships passing by the islands. They struggled through the winter and into spring, and on 6 October, their spirits were raised when a ship was seen sailing by, but despite lighting fires and endeavouring to chase down the vessel in one of their quarterboats, the ship continued on its way, its crew unaware of their presence.

They made little model ships outlining their plight which they regularly launched with tin sails in the hope that someone might find one washed up or notice a reflection from the metal sail. They carved details into driftwood which they launched into the sea, kept afloat with inflated seal bladders, but all to no avail.

By summertime, seven months after the shipwreck, they decided on a desperate mission to seek help by attempting to reach New Zealand, 490 kilometres to the north.

Work began on preparing one of the quarterboats for the perilous journey. They decked the vessel over with sealskins and made a sail out of old canvas that had been used on the roof of a hut built by earlier castaways.

It was stocked with 130 litres of water stored in seal gullets, smoked seal and goat meat and some 20 dozen cooked seabird eggs. It was also equipped with a small stove, made by one of the crewmen, and some charcoal.

On 22 January 1867, all was ready, and four men — Bartholomew Brown from Boston, the First Officer of the *General Grant*; William Newton Scott of Shields, England; Andrew Morrison of Glasgow; and Peter McNiven of Islay — set off from Port Ross on their perilous voyage.

Their task was hopeless. They had no compass or chart or nautical navigation instrument of any sort, but their worst mistake was their belief that New Zealand lay east-north-east of the Auckland Islands, whereas the direction was in fact the opposite, a little to the west of north.

The four men left Port Ross with a south-westerly wind blowing, but that night the wind turned to a strong north-westerly with heavy rain which would have blown them in the wrong direction. On the Auckland Islands the next day, 23 January, the winds shifted south-west again and the weather cleared and remained like that for the next week, raising the hopes of the castaways, if the four had survived the first night's storm.

These four brave men were never seen again, and what became of them will never be known.

For the eleven left behind the struggle continued. On 3 September, Scotsman David McLelland, a 62-year-old crewman of the *General Grant*, died and was buried on a sand hill on Enderby Island.

On 19 November 1867, they sighted the cutter *Fanny* from Invercargill offshore, but again their attempts to draw attention to their presence failed and the ship sailed on. Two days later, however, just after 3 p.m. on 21 November, another ship came into view, the Bluff-based whaling brig *Amherst* which was sailing up the east coast of Auckland Island and around towards Port Ross, and this time they were seen.

The *Amherst's* captain recorded their discovery in the ship's log:

> *On sighting Enderby Island the man at the masthead observed a sail coming out from the beach towards the vessel, supposed to be the cutter Fanny, from Invercargill, but on a nearer approach it proved to be a ship's boat with six men in it, the boat boarded the vessel when the crew proved to be part of the survivors of the ship General Grant, wrecked at this island in May, 1866, these men reported three others and one woman on shore on Enderby Island; the men were taken on board and the boat in tow — on reaching the deck the unfortunate castaways appeared to be bewildered by excitement at their deliverance — the vessel was then worked up to the anchorage in Port Ross, at 10 p.m.*

One of the castaways described the arrival of the *Amherst*:

> *When we got alongside, the men threw a rope to us, and we clambered upon deck. Words are powerless to express the sentiments of joy which we felt on seeing ourselves at last delivered from the miseries and privations we had endured for the long period of eighteen months.*

The *Amherst* moored for the night in Port Ross but was unable to get to those still onshore because of a squall. The next day cleared, and a boat was sent to rescue those still onshore — three men and Mrs Jewell — and on 13 January 1868, 20 months after the wreck of the *General Grant*, the ten survivors were landed at Bluff.

The survivors were Mary Ann Jewell and Joseph Jewell (passenger and seaman), William Ferguson (crew), Frederick Patrick Coughey (passenger), Nicholas Allen (passenger), Cornelius Drew (crew), James Teer (passenger), William Murdock Sangilly (crew), Aaron Hayman — also known as A. Harpman — (crew) and David Ashworth (passenger).

Following their rescue, and after two similar episodes on the island earlier with the wreck of the *Grafton* (January 1864) and the *Invercauld* (May 1864), the New Zealand Government set up a network of depots with supplies for any future castaways and established regular patrols of the subantarctic islands.

Meanwhile, the lure of the gold aboard the *General Grant* has been a magnet for treasure hunters ever since with 36 known salvage attempts, the first in 1868 and all of them unsuccessful. But they have come at a cost — as of 2022, the death toll from the unsuccessful gold-hunting expeditions was around 90 people.

## General Grant rescue rafts

The efforts by the survivors to let the world know of their plight with their model boats and floating driftwood was not entirely without success.

In 1868, one of their two model ships was found on the beach at Rakiura Stewart Island, but by that time they had been rescued.

In 1871 a Melbourne newspaper reported that another had been found 'somewhere in New Zealand' but had found its way into an antique shop in Melbourne. It was a boat-shaped piece of wood with the words:

'Ship Gen. Grant, wrkd Auckland Isles, May 14, 18 – (last two figures illegible) – 10 survive on Enderbys, Dec. 1, 1867. Want relief.'

The newspaper believed the artifact was genuine because of it being 'thoroughly waterworn, and presenting all the appearance of having been immersed for years.'

Just how it finished up in a Melbourne antique shop, and what happened to it subsequently, is unknown.

Collection of the Southland Museum and Art Gallery, Accession Number: 83.3387

A third, pictured here, was about to be launched by the survivors when help arrived.

Carved into the deck are the words:

'Want Relief Ship Gen. Grant wrkd Auckland Islands May 14 1866 10 survive on Enderby Island Nov 67'.

This float is now part of the Southland Museum collection. According to the museum the model was brought back with the rescued survivors on the *Amherst* and was displayed for some time in a shop or hotel window in Bluff before finally being gifted to the museum for safekeeping.

# 1891

# THE EAST COAST SEA SERPENT

New Zealanders were captivated in August 1891 by newspaper reports of the appearance of a giant sea serpent between Gisborne and Napier.

The first sighting was made east of Portland Island just off Māhia Peninsula, by crewmen of the Union Steamship Company passenger steamer *Rotomahana*, a 91-metre ship built in Scotland in 1879, and capable of carrying 332 passengers. It was known as the 'greyhound of the Pacific' because it was the fastest ship in Australasian waters and was the first ocean-going vessel in the world built of steel.

The ship was on a voyage from Auckland to Lyttelton via Gisborne, Napier and Wellington, carrying about 40 cabin passengers and with another 22 in steerage. It sailed from Gisborne Harbour on the afternoon of Friday, 31 July 1891 and was scheduled for its next stop at Napier the next day.

Just after 6.30 a.m. on Saturday, 1 August, the *Rotomahana* was steaming southwards in rough seas but in clear, sunny weather, when the Chief Officer, Alexander Kerr, stepped out onto the deck. To his astonishment, he saw a huge object rise out of the sea about 100 metres away from the ship.

He later described the sighting in graphic detail, saying it resembled a huge conger eel with a girth of about 12 feet (3.6 m) and with two large white fins about 10 feet (3 m) long, and had a white belly. He said its 'head did not appear to be particularly defined, the neck running right up to the head the same as a large eel'. He thought it was heading straight towards the ship.

The creature rose about 30 feet (9 m) out of the water, and Kerr said when it went beneath the water again, 'it did not fall forward like a fish that is jumping but drew itself back as if with a contortion'.

He said had the sea not been so rough, the *Rotomahana* might have endeavoured to get alongside the apparition to ascertain its length.

Kerr said he had been at sea for 27 years and had been:

> *engaged in nearly every known trade from whaling in Greenland to the slave trade, and have been in every part of the world, but I never saw any object at sea like the one that rivetted my attention on Saturday morning last.*
>
> *I have always been sceptical with regards to the sea serpent stories I have heard and read . . . but I have been too long at sea and seen too many remarkable things to deny positively that there is no such thing. I am too much accustomed to the sea however, to have made any mistake.*

The ship's Quartermaster, Peter Nelson, also saw the object. Nelson is described in contemporary newspaper reports as 'an intelligent, hard-headed seaman, not at all likely to be imaginative'.

He had just finished his shift as helmsman for the *Rotomahana* and had stepped out onto the deck on a bright sunny day, when he also saw the object rise up 30 feet (9 m) out of the heavy sea.

When it went down, he also said it didn't go forward like a fish jumping but seemed to draw itself back under the water as if it contracted itself.

He saw the object do this four times, the first time about a mile away and the last —about two minutes later — only about 100 yards from the ship.

'It looked like a huge conger eel or snake,' he said, 'except that it had two large fins. The fins seemed to be about 10 feet long and were situated about 20 feet from the head. The belly and the fins were pure white. I saw the back part. It was the colour of an eel.'

He dismissed suggestions that what he had seen might have been a whale, saying he had been at sea long enough to recognise them, and had it been at all like a whale he would have taken no notice of it.

'It was no more than 100 yards away the last time I saw it,' he said. 'The thing was glistening in the sun. Every time it went down there was a distinct splash that could be heard quite plainly.'

Like the First Officer, Nelson said he had often heard stories of sea serpents which he dismissed. He had never seen one himself, until this event, which had changed his mind. He declared:

> *Call it what you like, but after my experience of Saturday morning I am decidedly of the opinion that what I saw is a fish or creature that is never hardly seen. I never saw anything like it before, although I have been at sea 25 years, and have seen a great many queer things.*

When the *Rotomahana* arrived in Wellington the following day, they learned that an earthquake had been felt in Napier at 6.30 a.m. on Saturday, about the same time as they had seen the serpent, and Nelson was of the view that some disturbance at the bottom of the sea had 'caused the animal to come to the surface'.

After the supposed sea serpent sighting had been widely reported in newspapers, another witness came forward with his account of the phenomenon, which was published on Wednesday, 5 August.

Auckland surveyor Alfred Matthews said that nine days before the *Rotomahana* sighting, he was travelling from Auckland to Gisborne aboard the Union Steamship Company passenger steamer *Manapouri* when he and other passengers saw something that they later believed was the Portland Island sea serpent.

Their sighting was made 'a few miles' north of East Cape, north of

Gisborne. Between eight and nine o'clock in the morning of Friday, 24 July, he and other passengers and the ship's officers spotted the serpent about half a mile (800 m) away.

They watched it for more than ten minutes and said it was travelling along slowly, and every few minutes, would raise itself 20 or 30 feet (6 to 9 m) out of the water.

Matthews wrote that:

> *It would from time to time lift its head and part of its body to a great height perpendicularly, and when in that position turn its body round in a most peculiar manner, displaying a black back, a white belly, and two armlet appendages of great length, which appeared to dangle about like a broken limb on a human being. It would then suddenly drop back into the sea, scattering the water in all directions. It had a flat head, and was about half a mile distant from the ship.*

His description was confirmed by other passengers on the *Manapouri*.

Matthews said he had been reluctant to make public his observations because he was afraid that people would treat it with derision.

Doubts about the claims that the object was a sea serpent began to increase three weeks later, however, when Captain McLean, the master of the brigantine *Gleaner*, reported seeing something resembling a sea serpent about 100 miles (160 km) off Portland Island.

The 115-ton sailing ship was on a voyage from Napier to Auckland with a cargo of potatoes and flour, when on Sunday, 19 August, McLean and his crew sighted something in the water which they believed was the object seen by those aboard the *Rotomahana* and the *Manapouri*.

The sighting wasn't reported until a week later on 27 August when they finally arrived in Auckland after a stormy two-week voyage.

McLean said that when first spotted, the object was about 30 yards (27 m) away from the *Gleaner*, and from that distance it appeared 'very like a great snake'. But when they got closer, they could see that it was in fact a large tree, curved and twisted in shape, about 40 feet (12 m) long and 4 feet (1.2 m) in circumference that bore a 'striking resemblance to a semi-submerged serpent'.

'The largest part at one end was shaped like a fish's head,' he said, 'and the other like the flukes of a whale, the bark being stripped off in places, giving it a variegated appearance. It was in sight for two hours, rising and falling on the waves.' McLean continued:

> *The particoloured body, so carefully described by those who saw 'the serpent', might easily be accounted for by the fact that large blotches and strips of bark had been knocked off here and there, while the general contour of the broken projecting branches and jagged ends would furnish a rude resemblance to anyone seeing them from a distance to the head, tail, or flippers of some great saurian.*

McLean believed it was the contorted stem of a rātā tree and could understand why anyone seeing it from a distance could have mistaken it for some great aquatic snake or similar animal.

Plesiosaurus dolichodeirus, *the creature most like the Portland Island sea serpent.*
Artistic impression by Dmitry Bogdanov, Wikimedia Commons

While the sightings of a reported sea serpent fired the interest of the public, it didn't impress the scientific minds of the time.

Professor Frederick Hutton, professor of biology at Canterbury College (which in 1933 became the University of Canterbury) believed the object was a large tree that had been washed into the sea from a river.

He thought the description of the First Officer, Peter Nelson, that the object 'did not go forward like a fish jumping, but seemed to withdraw itself right back under water, as if it contracted itself,' could be accounted for by the tree bobbing slowly up and down in the water, or by waves rising and falling about it.

'As for the appendages and colour, some old trees are just as white as conger eels, and roots or branches could be conjured into flappers by distance and uncertain motion,' he reasoned.

'Besides this, if the sea monster had great fins or flappers, they would no doubt be used for the purpose of swimming, and it would be improbable that the creature would wave them about in the air like wings.'

Another leading scientist of the time, Sir James Hector, was also sceptical.

Hector was a Scottish-born surgeon, geologist and naturalist and remains one of New Zealand's foremost scientific minds. He served as the Chief Government Scientist, was manager of the New Zealand Institute (now the Royal Society of New Zealand), Chancellor of the University of New Zealand, President of the Royal Society of New Zealand and was elected a Fellow of The Royal Society.

He gave little credence to the belief that the object was some sort of sea serpent, dismissing it as a tree.

He said animals similar to the description given by the witnesses aboard the *Rotomahana* and the *Manapouri* had existed in New Zealand centuries before, as the discovery of their fossilised remains proved, but they were long extinct.

The descriptions of the Portland Island sea serpent are very similar to a prehistoric marine creature called a plesiosaurus that lived in the early Jurassic period, some 200 to 145 million years ago. It became extinct about 66 million years ago, at the time of the Cretaceous–Paleogene mass extinction event in which 75 per cent of plant and animal species on Earth became extinct.

The existence of plesiosaurs and other marine reptiles in New Zealand has been known from the fossil record since the 1860s.

# 1945

# OUR CLOSE BRUSH WITH NAZI WAR MACHINES

By January 1945, the Second World War had been raging for five and a half years, but the end was in sight.

The German Army was in retreat in Italy and Europe, Soviet forces were advancing on Poland and had seized Warsaw, Japanese forces were in retreat and American aircraft were bombing Tokyo.

For New Zealanders who had lived with the fear of a Japanese invasion since the attack on Pearl Harbor in Hawaii in December 1941, which intensified with the fall of Singapore in February 1942 and the air raids on Darwin that same month, life was looking a lot more positive.

But what Kiwis didn't know then was that one of Nazi Germany's most lethal war machines — the submarine *U-862* — was cruising our coastline in search of targets.

The submarine, described as 'the nastiest underwater weapon in the Nazi arsenal', spent almost a fortnight cruising our coastline and checking out various ports for targets, and all the time New Zealanders had no idea of its presence, officially or unofficially.

*U-862* was what was known as a Type IXD2 submarine. They had been designed in the mid-1930s as large ocean-going vessels capable of sustained missions far from their support bases. *U-862* was built in Bremen and launched in October 1943, with Kapitänleutnant Heinrich Timm as its captain. In its twelve months of operation, the submarine undertook two extended patrols and was responsible for sinking seven ships, none of them during its two weeks in New Zealand waters. But that wasn't for lack of trying.

It set out from Germany on its first patrol in May 1944, sailing to Penang in Japanese-occupied Malaya, which was the base for German submarines in South East Asia. It torpedoed five merchant ships off Africa en route and managed to shoot down a Royal Air Force Catalina seaplane. It also narrowly missed blowing itself up when it launched an acoustic homing torpedo at an oil tanker, but the torpedo went round in a circle and homed in on *U-862* instead. Only an emergency crash dive and complete silence saved it from its own torpedo.

*The Nazi Germany Type ICX/40 submarine, U-805, similar to U-862 which was a Type IXD2 vessel. U-862 was longer and heavier that the ICX/40 submarines. Each had six torpedo tubes, four at the bow and two at the stern, and could carry 22 torpedoes. This photograph was taken of U-805 as it was escorted to the Portsmouth Naval Shipyard in New Hampshire (USA), in May 1945 just a few days after the surrender of Germany.*
US Navy, Wikimedia Commons

Its second patrol began in December 1944 from Japanese-controlled Batavia in Dutch East Indies (now Indonesia), from whence it cruised down the west coast of Australia, across the Great Australian Bight and around the southern tip of Tasmania towards Sydney where on Christmas Day the US Liberty ship *Robert J Walker* was torpedoed. The ship was carrying 8600 tons of chrome ore used in the production of stainless steel. There were no survivors from its 68-man crew.

*U-862* then left the Australian coast and headed for New Zealand in search of more targets, rounding Cape Rēinga on 7 January 1945 and travelling down the east coast of the North Island. On 9 January, the submarine shadowed what it called a 'medium-sized steamer' for six hours off Cape Brett south of the Bay of Islands before losing the ship, apparently when it entered a harbour.

It continued southwards and on 13 January shadowed a coastal freighter en route from Auckland to Wellington off East Cape north of Gisborne. The submarine moved in to torpedo the freighter but couldn't complete the attack before dawn broke, when it withdrew for fear of being discovered.

The next day *U-862* watched a small steamer of about 600 tons sail from Gisborne Harbour, but the captain again decided against destroying the ship because it would have given away their presence. That night the submarine quietly entered Gisborne Harbour, where crewmen later said they watched cars driving along the roads and could see people walking along the streets, before it slipped away to sea undetected, heading south towards Napier.

There is an urban myth that German sailors from *U-862* went ashore during the night when the submarine was in Gisborne to steal fresh milk from a nearby dairy farm. However, it seems this did not happen, but arose from a joke that Heinrich Timm made to an RAF officer in the late 1950s.

On the evening of 15 January, the submarine was stationary on the surface just off Napier. The crew could hear a band playing and watched couples dancing in a promenade café. Early the next day the submarine followed a small steamer out of Napier Harbour, probably the coastal cement carrier *Pukeko* which had just discharged a cargo at Napier, and came close to another small ship just off the city, neither of which was aware of the presence of the Germans.

As *Pukeko* steamed up the coast towards Whangārei, *U-862* launched a torpedo at the ship, but the torpedo missed its target. The submarine, believing that it had been seen by the ship, left the area and headed south. There is no record to support the captain's belief that their attack had been seen by the ship's crew. The logbook of the *Pukeko*, which could have resolved the issue, was lost in a fire in the 1960s.

*U-862* crossed over Cook Strait on 19 January, about which time it was ordered to return to base. It continued down the east coast of the South Island still undetected, rounding Rakiura Stewart Island on 21 January and then headed back towards Batavia.

It claimed another victim on its return voyage, torpedoing the US Liberty ship, *Peter Silvester*, off Fremantle. It was carrying 2700 tons of supplies for the US Army along with 317 mules and 107 GIs destined for Burma. Thirty-three men died in that attack.

When Germany surrendered in May of 1945, *U-862* put into Singapore where it was taken over by the Japanese Navy and became *I-502*. And when Japan surrendered in August 1945 following the atomic bomb attacks on Hiroshima and Nagasaki, the submarine was seized by the Allies and scuttled in the Straits of Malacca in February 1946.

*U-862* was 88 metres long and could submerge to a depth of 200 metres. It was powered by two 9-cylinder diesel engines for surface travel and two electric motors for use while submerged. The U-boat could travel at 20 knots on the surface and seven knots submerged. It was fitted with six torpedo tubes and carried 24 torpedoes as well as four deck guns. It had a crew of 55.

It wasn't the only Axis vessel to enter our waters during the Second World War. Three German surface raiders were active here in 1940 and 1941: *Orion*, *Komet* and *Adjutant* were responsible for sinking three ships: the New Zealand Shipping Company freighter *Turakina* (20 August 1940) with the loss of 37 crew and 20 taken prisoner, the *Holmwood* (25 November 1940) with no loss of life, and the New Zealand Shipping Company liner, *Rangitane* (27 November 1940). Sixteen people were killed in that attack, eight passengers and eight crew.

Two other vessels were destroyed by mines laid by the German raiders. The liner *Niagara* was sunk by a mine off Whangārei on 19 June 1940 with no loss of life, and the minesweeper HMNZS *Puriri* was sunk by a mine in the Hauraki Gulf on 14 May 1940 with the loss of five crewmen.

The *Adjutant* laid magnetic mines at the entrance to Lyttelton and Wellington harbours in June 1941, a fact that only became known through secret German documents that were captured in 1945. The mines have never been found and it is assumed that they have sunk and become buried in seabed mud. A few days after laying the mines the *Adjutant* developed engine problems and was scuttled by its crew off the Chatham Islands, with the crew boarding another German ship.

Four Japanese submarines are known to have entered our waters: *I-29* in February 1942, *I-25* in March 1942, *I-21* in May 1942 and an unidentified submarine in February 1943. Floatplanes from the first three flew over Wellington, Auckland and Thames, but apart from causing widespread panic among the population, they had no other impact.

# Courage
## and
# Endeavour

# 1826

# HORRORS OF CANNIBALISM DETER FIRST SETTLERS

The first European attempt at organised settlement in New Zealand was a failure, apparently because the settlers were scared off by the reactions of the 'ferocious natives' to their presence.

The proposed settlement was the concept of the first New Zealand Company, which was formed in London in 1825. It was headed and chaired by Englishman John George Lambton, an ex-10th Hussars soldier and prosperous landowner whose wealth came mainly from mining in County Durham. He was also a Whip MP, a leading reformer of the time, a colonial administrator and diplomat, and was later raised to the peerage as 1st Earl of Durham.

The company had sixteen directors including four merchants of the East India Company, a merchant director of the Hudson Bay Company (who once owned 300 slaves on Caribbean sugar plantations), an economist, a Royal Navy officer, a banker, a writer, a solicitor, a shipping insurer and a number of politicians.

Like other entrepreneurs of the era, the directors could see potential

*Englishman John George Lambton, chairman and head of the first New Zealand Company formed in London in 1825. Lambton was an ex-10th Hussars soldier and prosperous landowner, a Whip MP, a leading reformer of the time, a colonial administrator and diplomat, and was later raised to the peerage as 1st Earl of Durham.*
Wikimedia Commons

profits from harvesting New Zealand's resources such as flax, timber, seals and from whaling around the coast.

In March 1825, Lambton and another director, Edward Littleton, met with the British Secretary of State for War and the Colonies, Lord Bathurst, to seek support for their plan.

The company asked for exclusive trading rights for New Zealand for a term of 31 years, and for a military force to provide protection 'from the natives' for its New Zealand settlements, both of which were refused. There was, nevertheless, a level of support for the company's plans, as evidenced by the fact that the president of the British Board of Trade, William Huskisson, had given the scheme his blessing. The following year Huskisson became Secretary for Colonies, and he is remembered today as the world's first railway passenger casualty, having been run over and fatally injured by Robert Stephenson's pioneering locomotive during the opening of the Liverpool and Manchester Railway in September 1830.

Despite the refusal, the company decided to push ahead with its plans, and it raised £20,000 to finance the establishment of agricultural and commercial trading settlements in New Zealand.

The company employed James Herd to head its expedition and secured two ships, the *Rosanna* and the *Lambton*. Herd was in command of the *Rosanna* and surveyor Thomas Barnett was employed to captain the *Lambton*.

Herd was an experienced sea captain who had visited New Zealand previously and traded with Māori. In 1821 he was in command of the *Providence* which left England for Australia on 6 June with 103 women convicts — 53 went to Hobart and the remaining 50 were taken to Port Jackson (Sydney). Also on board were a number of passengers travelling as free settlers.

They arrived at Port Jackson on 7 January 1822 and Herd spent the next two and a half months there. On 26 March he left for the Bay of Islands, arriving on 8 May. Two days later he left again for Hokianga, taking with him the missionary Thomas Kendall as an interpreter.

They spent four months there trading with the locals, swapping muskets and powder for 500 to 600 kauri spars and masts.

Herd also surveyed the harbour and its entrance, and he drew the first map of the harbour and surrounding land. On 7 August 1822, he signed an agreement with local chiefs Eruera Patuone and his brother Nene for the purchase of 40,000 acres (16,000 ha) of land around the harbour. The agreed price for the sale was 36 axes.

Patuone later gave his protection to New Zealand Company settlers at Hokianga.

*Providence* sailed again for the Bay of Islands in August 1822, and it headed for England on 4 September. Also on board was eighteen-year-old Thomas Surfleet Kendall, the eldest son of the missionary Thomas Kendall. London-born young Thomas had spent nine years in Northland from 1814.

Herd's ship for the New Zealand Company expedition, the *Rosanna*, was a 260-ton sloop with the hull sheathed in copper. The *Lambton* was a 62-ton cutter, a small, fast, single-masted vessel which the company hired from its Australian owner. Nothing is known of the crew of either ship.

*Missionary Thomas Kendall, from an oil painting by James Barry, 1820.*
Ref: G-618, Alexander Turnbull Library, Wellington, New Zealand

On 27 August 1825 the *Rosanna* left London with 38 passengers and a huge supply of the provisions they would need to establish themselves in their new settlement. It arrived at Torbay on 5 September and is believed to have finally departed England on 13 September. The *Lambton* left Torbay about 27 September, also loaded with supplies and 21 intending settlers.

Among the passengers were six officials of the New Zealand Company — an agricultural superintendent, a marine surveyor, two clerks, a surgeon and an interpreter. Other passengers included carpenters, blacksmiths, stonemasons, wheelwrights, bakers, shoemakers, ploughmen and gardeners.

Most were Scots, although there were a few from neighbouring Cumberland. They were chosen for the expedition by the agricultural superintendent, Thomas Shepherd, a nurseryman and surveyor. He spent the months of June and July 1825 interviewing applicants, and apparently had little difficulty recruiting the skilled people required for the expedition. He insisted on obtaining personal references as to the character of each of the applicants.

Thomas Surfleet Kendall joined the expedition as interpreter, apparently forgoing his training as a carpenter.

Six months later, on 5 March 1826, both the *Rosanna* and the *Lambton* arrived at Rakiura Stewart Island. They spent the next month there searching for a prospective settlement site and refitting the vessels.

Thomas Shepherd was initially enthusiastic about the island as a potential site for a settlement. He recorded encounters with a party of desperate seal hunters who had been left at the island by a Sydney trader months earlier and who had run out of supplies, and with a tattooed fellow Englishman who was living with local Māori. He also encountered a few of the island's Māori inhabitants.

But finally he concluded that Stewart Island offered nothing as a potential settlement site because there were insufficient resources to sustain them. Disillusioned, they left on 17 April bound for Otago Harbour, known at that time as Port Oxley, arriving there on 4 May 1826 after being held up at the heads for two days by contrary winds.

No sooner had the *Rosanna* dropped anchor than a fleet of waka containing some 100 local Māori turned up, apparently keen to trade. The next day trading did indeed take place, which seems to have been conducted to the satisfaction of both sides.

Shepherd and the company surveyor, Richard Bell, set out to explore the land around the harbour and were 'agreeably surprised' with what they found, resembling as it did parts of rural England. But they weren't totally happy with it and on 12 May, they set sail for Banks Peninsula where once again contrary winds prevented them from entering the harbour, and they sailed on towards Cook Strait.

Cloudy Bay to the east of present-day Blenheim, was the next spot to attract their attention. They dropped anchor there on 19 May and Shepherd, Bell and Herd went ashore to explore possible settlement sites.

Shepherd wrote that the land looked reasonably fertile, there was adequate fresh water and an excellent harbour. But they weren't impressed with the locals, whom he described as 'miserable looking creatures' who received them with 'a good deal of indifference'.

He wrote: 'We did not dread any injury they would do us as we were well armed and on our guard.'

It is a generally held view now that Shepherd's observations of the Māori inhabitants of the places they had visited indicated one of the main reasons for the failure of the expedition: an underlying fear of the threat that Māori represented to possible European settlement in their vicinity.

Returning to the ship, they decided once again that they were not impressed with what they had seen and agreed to move on. On 25 May they headed across Cook Strait and entered what they called 'Wanga Neu Atra', also known as Te Whanganui-a-Tara, now known principally as Wellington Harbour. The *Rosanna* struck some underwater rocks as it sailed into the narrow entrance to the harbour but escaped serious damage.

The *Rosanna* and the *Lambton* became the first European ships to enter Wellington Harbour. Herd named it Port Nicholson after his friend John Nicholson, harbourmaster at Port Jackson.

Once again Shepherd and Herd went ashore, possibly at what is now known as Worser Bay, near Seatoun. They traded with local Māori whom they described as 'civil' and over the next few days Shepherd, Bell and Herd explored the land around the harbour. They met and ate with some of the locals, but once again found the reception uncertain.

After presenting the inhabitants with fishhooks as gifts and looking around with the chief as their guide, Shepherd recorded that 'He went with us up the left branch [of the river] and when we returned neither he nor his people were so agreeable as before.'

He felt the harbour had potential as a settlement site but once again it wasn't exactly what they were looking for, and the decision was made to continue on northwards.

There is no record of the next few days and the voyage north, but it is known that on 23 June they entered Tauranga Harbour, becoming the first European ships to do so. They also visited Mercury Bay and the Firth of Thames, spending almost three months at the River Thames, now the Waihou River, near the present-day town of Thames.

They considered the area a serious contender for a settlement, but finally were driven away by their fear of the natives.

The missionary William Williams later recorded that Herd had told him of their experiences at Thames, recording that they had examined 'the different harbours on the coast, at length arriving at the river Thames, where they remained for fifteen weeks, and there they would have established themselves had they not been intimidated by the natives'. Māori at first were 'very civil, but at length they began to form designs against the vessels, which most likely would have succeeded had not the people been much on their guard'.

The French navigator Dumont d'Urville wrote in March 1827 that the settlers found the Hauraki site suited their aims, but 'hearing that the natives had made a plot to attack them without any warning and carry off everything they had brought with them, the new settlers fled with all speed'.

They set sail once again, this time for the Hauraki Gulf where they almost succeeded in establishing themselves.

On 23 September 1826, while the two ships were anchored off Waiheke Island, Shepherd, Bell and Herd signed a contract with local Māori for the purchase of 'Pakatu' (Pakatoa), 'Taratora' (Rotoroa), 'Ponue' (Pōnui) and 'Pake' (Pakihi) Islands in the Hauraki Gulf. The Company was planning to build a fort on Pakihi Island as a base for the settlement.

The purchase price was recorded as a barrel of gunpowder, eight muskets and one double-barrelled shotgun.

It appears that part of the reasoning behind the purchase was the expedition's belief that iron ore was abundant on Pakihi Island, which some believe was based on the presence of brown jasperoid which they mistook for iron ore.

At the time there was a lot of tribal warfare taking place around the Waitematā and the settlers, seeing evidence of cannibal feasts and observing many waka laden with ferocious-looking warriors, and witnessing warriors performing haka, once again decided against attempting to settle. They reportedly onsold the islands and left for the Bay of Islands where they arrived on 26 October 1826.

Herd and the others were clearly starting to despair of finding a suitable site to settle. Missionary Henry Williams, who welcomed the fleet to Paihia, recorded that in his meeting with Herd the next day the captain seemed to 'despair of success'.

'. . . they have not landed to remain any time, as the natives behaved with hostility towards them and felt disposed to take the vessels or to attack them. . .' he wrote.

By this time the company's investment had run up from the initial £20,000 to about £80,000 but the value of the flax they had harvested, which was to be offset against those expenses, was estimated at less than £20,000. Clearly financial problems were looming.

On Sunday, 26 November 1826, the *Rosanna* and *Lambton* once again set sail, this time heading for Hokianga which Herd had visited and mapped four years earlier.

They entered the harbour and sailed up the Hokianga River, and by 26 January 1827 they were at anchored at a spot that became known as Herd's Point, the location of present-day Rāwene, and there Herd entered into an agreement with the local chief Muriwai to purchase an area of land for their settlement. The payment for the land, listed in the sale agreement, included five muskets, 53 lbs (24 kg) of gunpowder, eight blankets, 300 flints, and four musket cartridge boxes.

But continuing disquiet over the locals once again interfered with their plans and this time it was intertribal warfare that was involved.

On 10 January 1827, the Ngāpuhi chief Hongi Hika attacked Ngāti Uru and Ngāti Pou at Whangaroa, and at some point the battles spread to Hokianga. The fighting was the final straw for the nervous settlers. They convinced Herd to abandon the New Zealand settlement dream and leave Hokianga in favour of the much more peaceful Port Jackson in Australia.

The *Rosanna* and the *Lambton* departed Hokianga on 30 January 1827, leaving one man behind, Alexander Grey, a blacksmith, who eventually took a Māori wife and lived independently at Hokianga.

The two ships arrived in Sydney on 11 February and the *Rosanna* eventually left Port Jackson for England on 15 June 1827, taking with it some of the disillusioned would-be settlers. A huge sale of the supplies that the intending settlers had taken with them on their voyage took place at Port Jackson in March 1827.

The *Lambton* was returned to its owner, Captain James Corlette, at Port Jackson and was operated by the Australian Agricultural Company. Its final fate is unknown.

Thomas Shepherd and some of the other families opted to remain in Australia, but four of the settlers, Thomas McLean, Benjamin Nesbit (a joiner), George Nimmo (a joiner) and Colin Gillies (ship's carpenter) eventually returned to Hokianga where they lived under the protection of the Ngāpuhi chief, Moetara Motu Tongapōrutu, a keen trader.

They joined another English settler, probably Alexander Grey, and all five men worked for the recently established Wesleyan mission station at Mangungu, repairing their boats and other equipment and carting supplies. They also apparently established a sawmilling business. The Wesleyan missionaries had established a settlement at Hokianga at the invitation of the chief Patuone after they had been forced to flee their first base at Whangaroa, which was sacked during Hongi's attack.

The New Zealand Company had proposed a second larger settler expedition to New Zealand but financial issues, and the failure of its first expedition, led to those plans being abandoned and the company ceased to operate.

But that was only the start of ambitious organised settlement schemes for New Zealand. In 1837 a second New Zealand Company was set up by Edward Gibbon Wakefield, which merged with the 1825 company, and also had Lord Durham as its chairman. The 1825 company claimed to own more than one million acres (4000 sq. km) of land in New Zealand.

This second New Zealand Company was eventually responsible for the settlement of more than 15,000 people in New Zealand in Wellington, Nelson, Whanganui and Dunedin, and was also involved in settlements in New Plymouth and Christchurch before winding up business, broke, in 1858.

# 1895

# ANTARCTIC FIRST
# FOR KIWI — MAYBE

On 24 January 1895, Alexander von Tunzelmann at the age of seventeen became the first New Zealander, and possibly the first person ever, to set foot on the Antarctic continent.

Alexander Francis Henry von Tunzelmann was born at the family home in Kawai Street, Nelson on 15 June 1877 to Johannes Emanuel and Eliza Philippa von Tunzelmann.

His Tunzelmann ancestors had emigrated from Prussia to Estonia where they were members of the Baltic German nobility, and therefore part of a privileged social class. His father Johannes, who went under the name of John, apparently emigrated to New Zealand along with a brother and sister in the 1850s, settling in Otago. In September 1869 he married Eliza Philippa Wheeler who was born in Saffron Walden in Essex. John died in the Seacliff Lunatic Asylum near Dunedin in 1898, aged 59, and Eliza died in Invercargill in 1921, at the age of 74.

John and Eliza had ten children and lived in Queenstown, Nelson, Christchurch and lastly Invercargill. Alexander was their fourth child and third son.

There is little information about his childhood and teenage years, but it is known that he was at Oban on Rakiura Stewart Island in November 1894 when the Norwegian whaling ship *Antarctic* sailed into port in search of crew. The 226-ton *Antarctic* was a Swedish-built barque with three masts and a steam engine and had been used on several research expeditions to the Arctic, but in 1893 it had been refitted as a whaling ship.

Its whale hunting expedition to the Antarctic Ocean was financed by Norwegian shipping and whale-hunting magnate Svend Foyn, who owned a fleet of whaling ships in the northern hemisphere and was expanding his business into the southern oceans.

The ship was captained by the Norwegian businessman and experienced whaler Henrik Johan Bull, with Leonard Kristensen as sailing master, and its complement included the Anglo-Norwegian polar explorer Carsten Borchgrevink.

*Antarctic* left Norway in September 1893 and headed to the Desolation Islands, a French-administered subantarctic island group in the southern Indian Ocean, one of the most isolated places on Earth and a popular whale- and seal-hunting area, where it hunted for the summer, moving on to Melbourne to sit out the winter of 1894.

It left there again on 26 September, calling briefly at Hobart and Campbell Island to resupply with fresh water, then headed for the Ross Sea and the southern whaling grounds on 7 November. But the voyage was cut short after the ship's propellor was damaged by ice, forcing it to

*Anglo-Norwegian polar explorer Carsten Borchgrevink claims he was the first man to step ashore on the Antarctic continent, a claim also made by New Zealander Alexander von Tunzelmann and the sailing master of the Antarctic, Leonard Kristensen. Borchgrevink was a pioneer of Antarctic exploration and in 1898–1900 led the British-financed Southern Cross expedition, which established a new Farthest South record at 78° 50'S.*

Quartermain Collection, Canterbury Museum

shut down its engine and head north under canvas to Port Chalmers for repairs. The ship was towed into Port Chalmers on 18 November, and two days later it entered the port's graving dock for repairs which were completed, and the ship refloated the next day.

Aboard the ship, however, all was not well with the 28-man crew. Two of them were arrested for drunkenness and appeared in the Port Chalmers Police Court on 21 November, and that night two others fled the ship, despite the officers maintaining a watch on board. The next day police arrested three more crewmen and charged them with drunkenness.

After restocking with coal on 22 November, *Antarctic* left Port Chalmers on 23 November for the Southern Ocean but left behind some of the crew who refused to sail. Shortly after, they stopped off at Stewart Island in search of replacement crew and that was when Alexander von Tunzelmann and three other New Zealanders, including Stewart Island whaler William Timaru Joss and another local, George Lonneker, were recruited to join what was to become an historic voyage. The name of the third crewman has been lost to history but it is known that he was a local Māori.

*Antarctic* was a lethal whale-hunting weapon, equipped with the latest technology for its bloody task. Its Norwegian sponsor, Svend Foyn, had patented a deadly new weapon in the industry — a grenade harpoon gun which revolutionised whaling — and the ship was armed with this latest technology.

The gun fired a barbed, explosive-headed harpoon which hooked into the whale, and was followed moments later by an explosive charge in the head of the harpoon which mortally wounded the whale. Using his technique, whales were then winched alongside the boat and pumped full of air to keep the body afloat until it could be processed, which happened alongside the ship.

Foyn's invention drastically changed the whaling industry which until then had been in the doldrums. It removed much of the danger traditionally involved with catching whales, and drastically increased the efficiency of the industry. It also made it possible to hunt all species of whale, including larger baleen whales like the 31-metre-long blue whale, the largest known animal to have ever existed, which hadn't been possible before.

*Antarctic* was equipped with eleven harpoon guns, a supporting arsenal of explosives and eight longboats.

The ship hunted seals around the subantarctic islands with success, but with few signs of whales, so they moved further south where whales had been reported by earlier expeditions. They sailed through a belt of pack ice into the Ross Sea and on 17 January made a landing on Possession Island off the north-eastern coast of Victoria Land in the western Ross Sea, north of McMurdo Sound. The British flag

*Norwegian entrepreneur and shipping magnate, Svend Foyn. His invention of the grenade harpoon gun in 1870 revolutionised the whaling industry.*

Norwegian Museum of Cultural History, CCO, via Wikimedia Commons

had been planted on the island in January 1841 by Captain James Clark Ross of the Royal Navy. They sailed north again and a week later on 24 January 1895 sighted land, later identified as Cape Adare, the northern tip of the Adare Peninsula, which is the most northern point of Victoria Land on the Antarctic mainland.

Sea conditions were relatively calm so Bull took the ship close to the shoreline and a longboat was lowered into the water. Seven men then took to the longboat and headed for the shore. That included the three expedition leaders — Borchgrevink, Kristensen and Bull — along with von Tunzelmann and three other crewmen.

Just who was actually the first person to step onto the shingle shore below the cape is disputed: Borchgrevink and Kristensen both later claimed that honour, and a drawing depicting the landing shows Borchgrevink in the lead.

But von Tunzelmann claimed right up until his death in 1957 that in fact he was the first person to step onto the southern continent, because he said he had 'leapt out to hold the boat steady' for the others to alight.

*This is a previously unpublished painting of the Norwegian whaler,* Antarctic. *It was a three-masted barque that was also equipped with a seven-horsepower auxiliary steam engine and had been built in 1871. The ship was lost after becoming trapped and badly damaged by pack ice in Antarctica during the 1901–04 Swedish Antarctic Expedition and sank on February 12, 1903.*

von Tunzelmann Family Archive

While ashore Borchgrevink collected specimens of rocks and lichens, which attracted a lot of interest from the scientific community on their return to Melbourne because until then, it had been the commonly held view that vegetation couldn't survive so far south. He apparently also closely studied the foreshore, looking for a suitable landing place for a future expedition.

Before 1895 other people had been close to or seen the continent but hadn't actually landed. In 1773 Captain James Cook and his crew in the *Resolution* crossed the Antarctic Circle for the first time, and while they sighted nearby islands and were within 240 kilometres of the Antarctic continent, they didn't physically see it because sea ice prevented them from sailing further south.

The first confirmed physical sighting of Antarctica occurred on 27 January 1820 when a Russian expedition led by Fabian Gottlieb von Bellingshausen and Mikhail Lazarev discovered an ice shelf at Princess Martha Coast, now known as the Fimbul Ice Shelf. They became the first people to discover the continent of Antarctica.

Von Tunzelmann and his bosses may not have been the first to actually land on the Antarctic continent. An English-born American seal hunter, Captain John Davis, claimed that he landed at Hughes Bay near the northernmost tip of the Antarctic Peninsula 74 years earlier on 7 February 1821 in search of seals. They found none and reportedly spent less than one hour on shore. His claim has never been authenticated.

The *Antarctic* expedition hunted about the Snares Islands, Solander Islands and Stewart Island for six months with limited success. They did kill one sperm whale that yielded four tons of oil, but not the right whales they were looking for, and they also caught 170 hair seals which produced about six tons of oil.

Newspaper reports from the time indicate the financial return from the expedition was a mere £300, well short of being a profitable enterprise. Henrik Bull described the voyage in an address to the Royal Geographical Society of Victoria as 'a great disappointment from the commercial point of view'.

Nevertheless, he believed there was a future for commercial whaling in the Southern Ocean if the right type of vessels could be deployed. Their expedition had not seen a single 'right' whale which earlier reports said were present in the area, but he said there were 'other species in sufficient numbers to justify a commercial enterprise'.

'A capital of £20,000 would provide three vessels of the proper type, which could take in one season forty whales,' he told the meeting,

*This drawing of the first landing in Antarctica shows Norwegian explorer Carsten Borchgrevink leaping ashore to become the first person to land on the continent. According to Alexander von Tunzelmann the depiction is inaccurate because he claimed he was the first person to set foot on the shore which he did so he could hold the boat steady for Borchgrevink and the two other expedition leaders, Leonard Kristensen and Henrik Bull, to step ashore.*

Paul Chaplin/NZHistory

*Alexander von Tunzelmann, taken at Invercargill on his 80th birthday in June 1957, shortly before his death on September 19, 1957. In 1984 the New Zealand Antarctic Place Names Committee officially named the Cape Adair landing spot Von Tunzelmann Point.*

von Tunzelmann Family Archive

'the produce of which would be worth £11,000 — a good enough return for the most exacting shareholder.'

Bull and Borchgrevink both left *Antarctic* on its return to Melbourne, but they later fell out, apparently over their differing accounts of the landing, each emphasising their own role in the event without acknowledging the role of the other. Both were keen to raise money to finance expeditions to explore the Antarctic, but neither succeeded, although Borchgrevink did later lead the 1898–1900 British-financed Southern Cross expedition which became the first to overwinter on the Antarctic mainland and established a Farthest South record.

Plans for the *Antarctic* to hunt whales and seals in the Southern Ocean were not universally welcomed. There were some in New Zealand who believed that the seas around New Zealand and its outlying islands should be protected 'against indiscriminate whaling on the part of foreign vessels'. They were worried that the revival of the whaling industry that the *Antarctic* represented would bring indiscriminate whaling by foreign vessels and they wanted the government to impose access restrictions on foreign whalers and to limit their catch. There was a strong feeling that New Zealanders should be the only ones allowed to hunt whales in

New Zealand waters to promote our own whaling industry as countries overseas had done to protect their seal- and whale-hunting industries.

After his Antarctic adventures, Alexander von Tunzelmann returned to Stewart Island and sometime in the early 1900s he married Elizabeth Adcock in Invercargill. The couple settled in a home that he had built in Kaipipi Road on Stewart Island.

They had five children, eventually moving to Invercargill about 1913 where he worked as a groundsman/gardener for Southland Boys' High School, living in a house on the school grounds. He also worked as a gardener at St John's Girls' School in Dee Street, Invercargill. Later they lived at 52 Baird Street, and he was employed by an Invercargill gardening company, believed to be Diacks Nurseries Ltd, which is still in existence. He and Elizabeth also purchased land in Lorne Street where they ran a large market garden and where Alexander constructed a number of clinker-built boats in a shed.

The family had one unsuccessful foray out of Invercargill, when they moved to Nelson where they planned to grow vegetables for the large Wellington market, but their plans were stymied by a waterfront strike which meant they couldn't get the produce to Wellington, and it rotted while waiting for the strike to end. After that mishap, they returned to Invercargill.

His grandson, Alan von Tunzelmann, recalls that Alexander was a keen outdoors man all his life, and was extremely fit through his hunting, tramping and fishing activities and from his gardening work. Alan says Alexander never owned a car, but did ride a motorcycle in his younger years, and he and Elizabeth cycled everywhere they went. One day while cycling to his market garden shortly after celebrating his 80th birthday, his bicycle's front wheel became entangled in twine and he tumbled off his bike, breaking his femur. He developed complications from that injury while in Invercargill hospital and died there on September 19, 1957.

Alan says his grandfather had a twinkle in his eye and the capacity to tell a good yarn right until the end of this life.

# Disasters and Accidents

# 1846

# THE NGĀTI TŪWHARETOA TRAGEDY

In the early nineteenth century, the Ngāti Tūwharetoa tribe — descendants of the legendary and powerful tohunga Ngātoroirangi who navigated the *Arawa* canoe to New Zealand — became the dominant iwi of the central plateau area of the North Island.

Their location in the middle of the island well away from coastal areas meant that they were largely isolated from European influence, at least until 1833, but they were well aware of the impact of Pākehā on the land and the effect of modern European weapons such as muskets on tribal warfare.

Their military and diplomatic activities in the 1820s and 1830s established the tribe as the principal iwi of the region with Te Heuheu Tūkino II, Mananui as the paramount chief.

The tribe had been based in the palisaded village of Waitahanui. This was not the present settlement of the same name just south of Taupō but was located near the mouth of the Tongariro River near present-day Tūrangi. For reasons that are unclear, Mananui abandoned the village when he became paramount chief during the 1820s and relocated to a new strongly palisaded pā, Te Rapa, just north of present-day Tokaanu near the geothermal area known as the Hipaua Steaming Cliffs — a decision that was to have tragic consequences.

Te Rapa was located just below volcanic hot springs on Mt Kākaramea, which was probably what attracted the iwi to the area.

On 6 May 1846, Mananui, his younger brother Iwikau and the rest of the iwi were preparing for the arrival of an ope, or travelling party, of Ngāti Maniapoto, probably from the Ngāti Te Kanawa iwi from the Taumarunui area. Heavy rain had been falling for some days. Missionary Richard Taylor recorded that the rain had caused a large landslide of clay and rocks on the mountain about 4 May which had dammed the flooded Waimataī Stream which drained the Hipaua Steaming Cliffs, creating a lake behind it.

The days of heavy rain also caused flooding in the Kuratau River a few kilometres north of Te Rapa, making the river impassable, and stranding the ope on the northern side, a chance situation that saved many lives.

The heavy rain continued into the night of 6 May and, according to Māori folklore, during a severe thunderstorm that accompanied the rain, Mananui climbed onto the roof of his whare, and armed with the Tūwharetoa heirloom known as Pahikaure, a greenstone mere, he called upon the spirits of the earth and sky for an end to the storm.

Legend records that he recited a number of prayers, including the karakia known as 'Kuruki whakataha' (evil, pass by), incantations that fell upon deaf ears.

The exact sequence of the events that happened next is a little unclear, but it appears that there was a second landslip which with a loud noise swept down the mountain, sending water, mud and debris into the village. But that was only a foretaste of what was to come, because minutes later a third and larger landslip crashed down the mountain, this time wiping out the dam left by the first landslide, and sending an enormous wave of rock, earth, trees and water thundering into the village, completely burying it and its occupants under 3 metres of mud. It is thought 63 people were killed including Mananui, his eight wives — four of whom were sisters — and his second son Te Waaka.

One person who escaped the carnage was Mananui's half-brother,

Tōkena Te Kerēhi. He had been disturbed by the noise of the landslide and went outside just as the flood of water and debris from the dammed Waimataī Stream crashed down onto the pā, but he escaped by running towards the lake and climbing up a tree.

An eyewitness, identified only as Kurauti, said later that after the second slip, Mananui Te Heuheu came out of the village's large wharepuni (sleeping house), but went back into the building in search of his son Te Waaka. It seems that took place only moments before the debris and flood of water from the destroyed dam hit.

The bodies of Mananui and his favourite wife, Nohopapa, were recovered and interred in a vault at Pūkawa between Tūrangi and Taumarunui, and later his body was taken to a burial cave on Mt Tongariro. In 1910 his remains were returned to Waihī village on the site of Te Rapa village by his grandson Wī Tamaiwhana and interred in a mausoleum in the village. Ironically, on 20 March 1910, Wī Tamaiwhana was killed by another landslide which hit the same area. It is said that he broke tapu by touching the body of Mananui.

*Te Heuheu Tūkino II (left) with his brother Iwikau behind him. The palisades of their pā, Te Rapa, near present-day Tokaanu, can be seen behind them.*
*From an 1844 painting by the English-born Australia painter, George French Angas.*
Wikimedia Commons

Te Heuheu Tūkino II, Mananui was apparently an impressive figure. The artist George French Angas described him as a man of imposing and dignified appearance, standing almost seven feet (just over 2 m) in height, with silvery white hair which his people compared to the snowy head of the sacred Mt Tongariro.

History recalls him as the most influential and respected leader in the central North Island and one of the most distinguished Māori leaders of the time, remembered for his wisdom and actions such as forbidding the practice of cannibalism.

His role as paramount chief of Ngāti Tūwharetoa was taken by his brother, Iwikau, who served as Te Heuheu Tūkino III, Iwikau, until his death in 1862.

# 1880

# WIND-BLOWN RAIL CRASH KILLS FOUR

The first fatal rail accident in New Zealand occurred on 11 September 1880, when five carriages and wagons on a Greytown to Wellington train were blown off the tracks by a severe gale.

The accident happened on a section of the line between Wellington and Greytown that was notorious for its high winds. At that time the railway climbed over the Rimutaka Range (spelled Remutaka from 2017) from Kaitoke at the northern end of present-day Upper Hutt city, to Featherston via what was known as the Rimutaka Incline. The part of the line where the accident occurred was officially known as Horseshoe Bend, but because of the cold, powerful winds, it was commonly referred to as Siberia.

The Wellington to Wairarapa railway line was built in the 1870s with the first section from Wellington to Kaitoke opened on 1 January 1878, and the extension over the Rimutaka Range to Featherston opened on 12 October that year.

It was an impressive engineering feat, tackling a 1-in-40 gradient on the Wellington side of the summit and a 1-in-15 gradient on the Wairarapa side. The line was the steepest in New Zealand, dropping

265 metres in just under 5 kilometres. It required the use of Fell engines to pull or slow the trains over the steep grades involved.

These engines were invented by the English railway engineer John Fell. They involved a specially built locomotive and a third rail positioned between the usual two rails, which was gripped sideways by an additional set of wheels under the engine's boiler; the wheels were held in place against the rail with compression springs. The system could be used to provide traction for ascending steep inclines or for braking on steep descents. The system in use on the Rimutaka Incline also used a special brake van with brakes operated by the guard.

The line from Kaitoke to Featherston was a major undertaking. It involved four tunnels (three straight and one curved), a large wooden truss bridge over the Pākuratahi River, many small bridges and culverts, and many cuttings and embankments. It included a large earth and rock embankment across Horseshoe (Siberia) Gully that linked Siberia tunnel and Price's tunnel. It also featured some of the tightest curves on

*This is one of the Fell H-class steam locomotives used on the Rimutaka Incline. This one is identified as number NZR 199, 0-4-2T.*

Godber, Albert Percy, Alexander Turnbull Library, public domain, via Wikimedia Commons

the New Zealand rail network, all of which meant severely restricted train speeds and engine loads. It was also subject to very strong winds.

On 11 September 1880, the Saturday morning train to Wellington left Greytown station at 8.30 with two carriages reportedly full of passengers, a luggage van, two goods wagons loaded with timber, and the brake van. It stopped at a point known as Cross Creek at the foot of the Rimutaka Incline just south of Featherston, where the regular engine was uncoupled and replaced by the Fell engine to pull the train up the 4-kilometre 1-in-15 ascent to the summit of the range.

The two carriages and the luggage van were in front of the engine, and behind it were the two goods wagons and the brake van. There was only a moderate breeze blowing when the train started its ascent, but the wind grew stronger as it climbed higher and when it was halfway up the incline, a gale was blowing with even stronger gusts encountered as it passed the numerous gullies.

Travelling at its usual speed of about five miles an hour (8 km/h) the train came out of Price's tunnel and around a rocky cutting on a steep hillside and onto an embankment bridging a deep gully. The embankment was constructed with earth and rocks that came from the cutting and from the nearby Siberia tunnel and was some 100 metres high on the downside of the gully.

The embankment was very exposed and was subject to almost continuous fierce, cold winds and powerful wind gusts.

As the train made its way across the embankment it was buffeted by a very strong nor-west gale. Then a sudden, even stronger gust hit, hurling the leading carriage off the rails onto its side, and taking with it the second carriage and the luggage van. As the first carriage toppled over, it smashed into the rocks along the side of the embankment, which tore off its roof and most of the bodywork, hurling passengers, rocks and wreckage from the bodywork down the steep side of the embankment.

The chassis of the wrecked carriage plunged over the edge of the embankment, pulling with it the second carriage and the luggage van. But fortuitously they remained intact, and the couplings joining them held together, leaving the three vehicles dangling down the incline at

*A Fell engine and train exiting Siberia Tunnel on the Rimutaka Incline photographed about 1910, 30 years after the fatal accident of 1880. High fences have been built as windbreaks on both sides of the railway line. The young boy sitting on the fence in right foreground is believed to be William Godber, son of the photographer, Albert Percy Godber.*

Ref: APG-0153-1/2-G, Alexander Turnbull Library, Wellington, New Zealand

right angles to the engine which remained on the rails with its four horizontal steel wheels firmly gripping the centre rail.

That powerful grip prevented what would otherwise have been a catastrophic disaster, had the engine and the other three wagons been pulled off the rails and the whole train crashed down to the bottom of the ravine on top of the carriages and the passengers.

The surviving passengers struggled down the steep embankment to provide what aid they could to the injured. More than 20 passengers had been hurt, some of them seriously, but it was children who suffered the worst.

Three were killed in the crash — eleven-year-old Ida Pharazyn (whose twin sister Ella survived but was badly injured), five-year-old William Quinn, and Francis Nicholas. A fourth child, Stanley Nicholas, a brother of Francis, died later from his injuries. The age of the two boys was given as three and seven.

As the survivors rendered what assistance they could to the injured, the train's crew uncoupled the brake van from the engine, allowing it to run back down the incline towards Featherston under its own momentum, with the guard using its brakes to control its speed. It was stopped at the Cross Creek station and from there a telegram was sent to Wellington alerting authorities of the accident. The telegram was delivered to the general manager of the Wellington and Greytown Railway at 10.30 a.m., about an hour after the accident.

The drama at the crash scene continued. The Fell engine was left swaying dangerously under the pull of the suspended carriages and the hurricane-force winds that continued to batter it. Finally, the two goods wagons, freed from the trailing brake van and only connected to the engine, also fell victim to the fury of the wind and they too were blown off the rails, toppling over but still coupled to the engine. That left the Fell engine still gripping the centre rail and supporting the three carriages in front and the two goods wagons at the rear.

In Wellington, meanwhile, a rescue mission was quickly assembled. A special train was organised to get help to the scene, and railway porters were sent to summon four local doctors who rushed to join the rescue mission. The relief train left Wellington at 11.30 a.m., with the party arriving on the scene at 1 p.m., a very quick response considering the difficulties of communications, the distances involved and the complexity of arranging a rescue.

From Cross Creek, another Fell engine and carriages were quickly organised to get help to the scene. Many of the injured were taken to hospitals in Featherston and Greytown, along with the bodies of the three dead children. Another train from the Hutt Valley carried more of the injured back to Kaitoke where they were treated by the doctors brought up from Wellington, and then taken by train back to the city hospital.

Shortly after this accident a fence was erected along Siberia Gorge to act as a windbreak, which proved to be very effective.

But it didn't stop the problem of wind blowing rail traffic off the Wairarapa line. On 8 October 1936, a strong nor-west wind blew a

16-tonne railcar off the rails near Pigeon Bush just south of Featherston. Ironically the railcar was about 20 metres short of a quarter-mile-long (440 m) windbreak intended to prevent such accidents.

The railcar, dubbed *Mamari*, had been especially built to handle the steep grades on the Rimutaka Incline, and at 16 tonnes was almost half the weight of the railcars used on other less challenging routes. It had left Masterton on the regular daily run to Wellington and had been buffeted by high winds after leaving Carterton. There were no concerns about it being blown off the track until it was hit by a severe gust thought to have been of about 80 miles an hour (125 km/h).

The railcar was carrying 24 passengers, and eight of them suffered broken bones while others were hurt by flying glass.

After the crash the guard was able to reach a nearby telephone and call for help, and a local doctor was on the scene shortly after. The injured were taken back to Featherston for treatment while another train returned the uninjured back to Greytown, Carterton and Masterton.

The railcar was returned to the rails later that day and towed by steam train to the railway workshops in Lower Hutt for repairs.

The Rimutaka Incline remained in operation until 30 October 1955, when the route was changed with the opening of the 8.8-kilometre Rimutaka Tunnel on 3 November 1955. At the time it was the longest tunnel in New Zealand, reducing the travel distance between Upper Hutt and Featherston from 40 kilometres to 25.

# 1886

# PHANTOM CANOE OR MANIPULATIVE FAKE?

Monday, 31 May 1886 dawned cool and sunny with a light mist across the waters of Lake Tarawera as a party of six European tourists were canoed across the misty lake towards the famed Pink and White Terraces on adjacent Lake Rotomahana.

The canoe was paddled by six or eight Māori — the number varies in different accounts — and they were escorted by the famed Māori guide Sophia Hinerangi, also known as Te Paea or, more familiarly, 'Guide Sophie'. She had been born at Kororāreka in the early 1830s and lived at Te Wairoa beside Lake Tarawera. She was the principal guide for the Pink and White Terraces tourist operation that attracted people from all over the world.

The terraces were believed to be the largest silica deposits of their type in the world and were described at the time as the Eighth Wonder of the World.

They were New Zealand's most famous tourist attraction but not too many European tourists visited them because to get to New Zealand from London took about 40 days by steamer. Once here, they usually travelled from Auckland to Tauranga by steamer, then by horseback to

Ōhinemutu on Lake Rotorua. From there it was horse and coach to Te Wairoa near Lake Tarawera (now known as the Buried Village) and then a canoe trip across the lake and a walk over the narrow strip of land that separates Lake Rotomahana from Lake Tarawera.

There were six European tourists on the canoe that day: Mr and Mrs Sise from Dunedin and their daughter, two men named as Dr Ralph and an Auckland man, Mr Quick, and a priest, also from Auckland, identified as Father Kelleher.

The canoe was about halfway across Lake Tarawera when another canoe described as 'a strange double-headed canoe, like a war canoe' with raised prow and stern posts and with about nine people on board, appeared out of the mist to the north of them and followed a course parallel to them, about 800 metres away.

The two boats journeyed along for some few minutes until the mysterious canoe disappeared behind a headland.

The problem was no one had seen a double headed war canoe on the lake previously and there was no memory of there ever having been such a canoe on the lake.

There are various accounts of the phantom canoe and its passengers.

The Māori paddlers aboard the tourist canoe described it as a war canoe with a double row of occupants, one row paddling and some of those in the other row standing, wrapped in flax robes with bowed heads and their hair adorned with feathers of the huia and the kōtuku (white heron). According to Māori custom huia feathers were worn to a tangi and used to adorn the hair of the dead.

They were convinced that the phantom canoe was carrying the souls of the dead towards a traditional Māori burial ground on the slopes of Mt Tarawera.

The Dunedin tourist, Mr Sise, said he counted nine people on the phantom canoe and that three of them had stood up as it moved through the water.

He said he could see the flash of paddles and counted three paddlers on the side nearest to him. He commented that their style of paddling indicated 'a fine muscular development'. He described the paddlers in

*The phantom canoe seen on Lake Tarawera on 31 May 1886, as visualised by the Indian-born artist Kenneth Watkins in this 1888 oil on canvas painting.*
Wikimedia Commons

his canoe shouting and whistling to the phantom canoe, but there was no reaction from those on board the strange craft.

The tourists didn't realise at the time what they were seeing so they were quite calm at the appearance of the second canoe, albeit a little mystified by the reactions of their paddlers. They admitted later that had they been aware their companion canoe was a phantom they would have been 'quite alarmed'.

To the Māori, however, its appearance was a portent of troubled times ahead. It added to their fears which had already been aroused earlier in the day as they were about to board the canoe when the waters of the lake mysteriously rose sharply, and then a few minutes later receded to normal levels. Reportedly that had happened on numerous occasions over the previous few days.

The paddlers were so concerned at that incident that initially they refused to board the canoe or go on the lake, but after some persuading they reluctantly agreed to carry on.

After visiting the terraces and enjoying the spectacle the tourists returned to Te Wairoa, where one said, '. . . to our surprise we found the Maoris in great excitement, and heard from McCrae [a permanent resident] and other Europeans that no such boat had ever been on the lake'.

According to the online *Te Ara — the Encyclopaedia of New Zealand*, there was a second tourist canoe on the lake at the same time and its occupants also saw the phantom canoe.

One of its passengers, named as Josiah Martin, is said to have sketched his impressions of the canoe. This would possibly have been the same Josiah Martin, a teacher turned photographer, who ran photographic studios and businesses in Queen Street, Auckland. He photographed topographical and ethnological subjects and was known to have visited Tarawera and Rotomahana in 1876, and he was in the area when Mt Tarawera exploded, photographing the aftermath.

Martin was well known in the nineteenth century for his topographical and ethnographical photography and regularly lectured in New Zealand and Britain on the subject, and on his scientific observations. His most important lecture, *The Terraces of Rotomahana, New Zealand*, was given to the Geological Society in London in 1887 and sealed his reputation as both a photographic and scientific observer. He won a gold medal for his photography at the *Exposition Coloniale* in Paris in 1889.

Several theories were advanced at the time for the mysterious appearance of the phantom canoe.

Sise believed it was a hoax, the work of a struggling local tohunga who was in need of something to reinforce his reputation with his followers.

'An ethereal canoe, manned by phantoms is a very impressive apparition if viewed with due reverence, and in fact it should be part of the stock-in-trade of any properly regulated prophetic establishment,' he said.

Others believed that the earlier sudden rise and fall in the level of the lake was caused by a pre-eruption fissure which had freed a burial waka from its resting place on the bottom of the lake. They said there was a tradition for the dead to be tied in an upright position in canoes which were then sunk.

Sceptics of the phantom canoe believed it was a freak reflection of the tourists' own canoe in the mist that was shrouding the lake, but elders of the Te Wairoa tribe believed it was a waka wairua — a spirit canoe — and a portent of doom.

As it was, doom did indeed strike ten days later on 10 June 1886 when Mt Tarawera erupted with unimaginable violence.

It began just after midnight when a series of earthquakes of increasing intensity shook the area and there was an unusual display of sheet lightning over the mountain. Huge explosions were heard about 1.30 a.m., and shortly after that at about 2.10 a.m., Mt Tarawera began exploding with spectacular violence, sending an eruption cloud high into the air. Shortly after all three peaks erupted, sending three distinct clouds of volcanic ash into the sky.

At about 3.30 a.m. the biggest explosion occurred when a fissure vent from which molten lava was streaming reached Lake Rotomahana. The lake water coming into contact with the magma caused an even bigger explosion which destroyed the lake and most of the famous terraces. It created a 2-kilometre-wide volcanic crater and spread tephra (material that falls from the sky after a volcanic eruption) over 10,000 square kilometres of the North Island, and it produced a pyroclastic surge (of gas and rocks) that destroyed all villages within a 6-kilometre radius.

It is thought some 120 people were killed, mostly Māori who lived in the villages. Some put the death toll at thousands.

The violent eruption lasted for about six hours, but material continued to be blown from the volcano for another ten days. Steam blasts continued for months afterwards until activity gradually came to an end and Lake Rotomahana began to refill, but without the famous terraces.

The noise of the eruption was heard as far away as Auckland in the north and Kaikōura in the south, and ash and debris fell up to 15 metres deep in the immediate vicinity.

Today, Te Wairoa — the buried village — is a popular and sombre tourist attraction.

The Tarawera Phantom Canoe is not the only reported omen of pending disaster.

In July 1931, stories began to emerge from the Chatham Islands of a mysterious phantom launch which appeared in the nearby fishing grounds prior to tragedy and loss of life.

Several fishermen reported seeing the mysterious vessel that month, and shortly after the 12-metre yawl-rigged (two-masted) Chatham Islands launch *Te Aroha* vanished with the loss of eleven lives.

The launch left Kāingaroa on the north-east end of Chatham Island (the main island) at midday on Friday, 17 July bound for Ōwenga, 38 kilometres to the south and also on the main island where the eleven men were to play rugby. But they never arrived, and the fate of the vessel wasn't discovered until Tuesday, 21 July, when wreckage was spotted at Point Munning just a short distance from where they had set out. There were no survivors.

Wreckage of the *Te Aroha* was found scattered around the coast of Chatham Island and as far away as Rangiauria Pitt Island 40 kilometres to the south.

The vessel had left Kāingaroa in heavy seas and a strong north-west wind which increased to gale force as the day wore on and continued for the next three days.

*Te Aroha* had apparently foundered in a rip tide and heavy following sea.

For the Chatham Islands' community the loss of the launch was a shocking tragedy. The dead were named as B. Remi, Joseph Paynter, William Paynter, Edward Thompson, Michael Thompson, Waiti Thompson, Bishop Ashton, James Whaititi, H. Stone, Ririmu Wiki and Taaka Ngaia, all residents of Kāingaroa and all Māori. The three Thompsons were brothers as were the two Paynters. William Paynter and Ririmu Wiki were married men with families. The others were all single.

*Te Aroha* had been built on the Chathams and was said to be 'one of the staunchest and most powerful' launches in the islands. Usually it carried three or four people.

Locals said the *Te Aroha* had probably foundered near Point Munning, which they described as a very dangerous part of the coast, especially in bad weather. They said the tides, rips and seas experienced there were far worse than anything encountered in Cook Strait.

The Chatham Islands phantom craft was again seen in August 1934.

On this occasion several fishermen claimed they saw the launch travelling at high speed, saying it appeared out of the mist in thick weather and passed without noticing them. They claimed it had been so close that they could see the engine working but they said there was no one on board.

One of those who reported seeing the apparition was Chatham Islands fisherman Samuel Nicholson who was a firm believer that the appearance of the phantom launch was a warning of an impending disaster.

In this case he was the victim. He fell out of his fishing boat a few days later in heavy seas and was drowned.

Others believe it was not a phantom launch at all but a poacher's boat, possibly American or Japanese, involved in illegal seal hunting out of season on the Chatham Islands. There were large numbers of seals on the Chathams, particularly of the species that produced the best quality fur.

# 1904

# NATURE BRINGS FAMILY TRAGEDY AT BRUNNER

The West Coast of the South Island has had more than its share of human tragedies and disasters.

The Coast is well known for its heavy rainfall, the result of the rugged topography of the area and its physical location which means moist air sweeping in from the Tasman Sea is forced up and over the Southern Alps, condensing the moisture into rainfall. The result is that the West Coast is one of the wettest places on Earth — in some parts of the region, rain falls at the rate of more than 13 metres a year.

Human activity often makes the situation worse. Steep hillsides stripped of their natural covering of bush and trees, which protected the land for millennia by filtering the run-off from these heavy rains, become prone to slips. Sometimes these slips are a mix of water, rock, soil and vegetation and resemble wet concrete, overpowering and burying everything in their path.

That's what happened at the West Coast mining town of Wallsend in the Brunner Gorge, inland from Greymouth in the early hours of the morning of 25 May 1904, with tragic consequences.

Wallsend was a mining settlement for the Brunner Mine which had been operating since 1864, and it was the commercial and service hub of the area. The township was a few kilometres downstream from the mine and on the other side of the Grey River where there was slightly more space for housing for the workforce. It was one of three dormitory settlements — the others were Taylorville and Dobson, and photos of the era show that the surrounding hillsides had been extensively cleared of their vegetation cover.

Thunder, lightning and heavy continuous rain hit the area on 24 May — Empire Day — causing widespread flooding, with the Grey River rising rapidly and slips occurring in many areas. At four o'clock that afternoon, a portion of the hillside behind the Wallsend shops crashed down into the J.W. Parkinson chemist shop and house, sweeping it down onto the road below, where it came to a halt in pieces. Debris from the slip carried on towards the river, crashing into two houses, knocking one off its foundations by a metre. The mud and debris continued its downward course till it hit the railway line, where it stopped, blocking the line, and stranding the Reefton passenger train behind it.

The chemist himself had a narrow escape. He and his family were aware of the danger posed by the steep hillside behind the building, and were leaving the property, but it seems Parkinson returned to the building to recover the shop's cashbox and was leaving again when the landslip hit, trapping him inside where he stayed until the splintered remains of the building came to a rest on the roadway.

But worse was to come.

At 2.30 in the morning the following day, 25 May, with heavy rain still falling, a second landslide thundered into the township, this time smashing into the Jones Terminus Hotel, demolishing one wing of the building and killing the owner, 60-year-old Henry Jones, who was sleeping in the wing. His three daughters, who were sleeping upstairs, escaped unhurt as did his son who was asleep in another area of the ground floor.

It seems that the hotel was saved from total demolition by a mound

*Rescue workers digging through the debris and remains of Jones' Terminus Hotel in the effort to recover the body of the owner, Henry Jones. Debris from the slip and wreckage of the hotel covered the main road in front of the hotel.*
Alexander Turnbull Library, Wellington, New Zealand

of solid rock on the mountain behind the building, which deflected the worst of the landslide away from the main structure of the building but tragically sent the full force of the clay, rocks and vegetation into a next-door cottage that was occupied by Walter and Ellen Cosgrove and their seven young children.

Walter Cosgrove was awakened by the crash of the landslide hitting the house, and he woke his wife who fled from the building carrying their two youngest children — four-year-old Nellie and eighteen-month-old Nora — while he rushed to the back of the house where their other five children were sleeping, only to find that portion of the house totally destroyed under tons of debris. The house was moving down the hill as he endeavoured to get out through the front door, but he was unable to do so, finally escaping through a broken window as the house and debris continued to slide, finally coming to rest about 10 metres further down.

Debris from the slip continued to pour down the hillside, overwhelming Mrs Cosgrove as she tried to escape, burying her up to her neck and smothering the two children in her arms.

Within minutes, hundreds of rescuers had descended on the scene in the dark and worked frantically by the light of lanterns to free her from the mud. She was clinging to the body of one child, and rescuers found the body of the second a short distance away. Both bodies were badly damaged, indicating the forces involved.

Mrs Cosgrove herself was badly injured and suffering from severe shock, but she survived, and was taken to a neighbour's house.

Rescuers then turned their efforts to the rear of the house where the other five children had been entombed. They cleared away tonnes of dirt, rocks, vegetation and wrecked building, and by 11 o'clock in the morning the bodies had been recovered.

The bodies of all seven children were taken to the Wallsend Courthouse where the local women had gathered to attend to them, washing them and laying them out on the courtroom floor.

A reporter from *The Greymouth Evening Star* wrote, in what was clearly a huge understatement, that the scene at the courthouse was 'a terribly sad one':

*The Cosgrove family cottage stood on the left side of this photograph. The only visible sign of the cottage is the few broken timbers in the left foreground. An enormous amount of debris and the wreckage of the building had been removed during the recovery of the children's bodies.*

Alexander Turnbull Library, Wellington, New Zealand

*As the miners brought one little body after another into the building the tension was terrible, yet it was noticeable how cool and collected a number of the women were as they took the sad load from the men and proceeded to clear the mud, undress and wash the corpses. It was a picture fit to touch a heart of stone to see the seven, all of one family, who but yesterday were in the full enjoyment of health laid out side-by-side, inanimate forms. Two bodies were greatly mangled, but the others were not so much bruised. The expression on some of the faces was calm and peaceful, showing that they had not suffered.*

The five dead elder children were thirteen-year-old Bessie, twelve-year-old Maggie, ten-year-old Mary, eight-year-old Thomas and five-year-old John. All seven children were buried in a mass grave at the nearby Stillwater Cemetery where their brother, Walter, who had died in 1898, was buried.

It wasn't Ellen Cosgrove's first brush with tragedy: her first husband, 38-year-old Patrick Casey, was killed when he fell in front of horse-drawn coal trucks on Brunner Bridge in June 1889.

*The reality of a terrible tragedy: the seven Cosgrove children lie in their coffins in the Wallsend Courthouse after the landslip. Sadly, the original photograph has been lost — only this grainy copy remains.*

Peter Ewen

The Cosgroves went on to have another child in 1905, a boy they named Joseph, who died in 1965.

The body of Henry Jones, owner of the Terminus Hotel, was recovered two days later and he was buried in the Greymouth Cemetery.

That storm caused widespread damage around the West Coast. A road and rail bridge upstream from Wallsend was washed out, there were numerous slips that blocked road and rail links, and a locomotive and two wagons were derailed.

# Enterprise

# 1796

# NEW ZEALAND'S FIRST LOCALLY BUILT SHIP

The first ship to be built in New Zealand set sail from Dusky Sound in Fiordland on 7 January 1796 with 90 castaways aboard, bound for Norfolk Island.

The 65-ton, 16-metre schooner was named *Providence* and had been started by a party of sealers who had been landed at Luncheon Cove on Anchor Island in Dusky Sound, but it had been abandoned by them when they were picked up for the return voyage to Sydney.

The twelve-man sealing party had arrived from Sydney in November 1792 aboard the ship *Britannia* under the command of Captain William Raven, with sufficient supplies to last them for a year while they went about the task of killing and skinning fur seals, New Zealand's first export industry. *Britannia* was owned by Enderby and Company, a British company which had a three-year licence from the powerful East India Company to trade in the area. There was strong demand for the skins at the time, particularly from China, because the fur is very dense and glossy, and can be easily dyed.

It was known that there was a vast population of seals in Fiordland after Captain Cook had in 1773 explored the sounds and feasted on seal meat. His log recorded:

*I went with a party a Seal hunting, (and) in one place where we killed Ten, these animals serve us for three purposes, the skins we use for our rigging, the fatt makes oyle for our lamps and the flesh we eat, their harslets [heart and liver] are equal to that of a hog and the flesh of some of them eats little inferior to beef steakes. . .*

On 14 November 1792, under the command of *Britannia*'s second mate William Leith, the sealers began to build a home for themselves on the shores of Luncheon Cove, so named by Captain Cook because he and his crew had enjoyed a lunch of crayfish there during their visit in 1773. The building was New Zealand's first European-style house and was a thatched-roofed structure measuring about 40 feet long and 15 feet wide (12 m by 5.5 m), along with an adjoining support building to store their supplies and as a space to dry the skins.

As well as providing the party with provisions and stores, Enderby and Company also supplied them with ironwork, rope, sails, a forge to work iron and a steambox which was used to bend cladding planks to fit the shape of the hull frame of wooden ships, along with instructions that they should use these items to build themselves a ship, just in case, for whatever reason, their pick-up ten months later didn't occur.

But it did: on 28 September 1793, the *Britannia* returned to Dusky Sound to collect the sealers and their haul of some 4500 sealskins, and they left the Sound to return to Sydney on 31 October, abandoning their two buildings and their partly built schooner.

But their shipbuilding work didn't go to waste, because on 10 October 1795 two other Sydney-based sealing ships arrived at Dusky Sound, the *Endeavour* and the *Fancy*, dropping anchor at Facile Harbour on Resolution Island. The *Endeavour* was an ageing three-masted 280-ton sailing vessel under the command of Captain William Bampton, while the *Fancy* was a 150-ton brig under the command of Captain E.T. Dell.

They had left Sydney on 18 September en route to Bombay via Dusky Sound where they planned to spend some time seal hunting but had only just cleared the coast when stowaways — 44 men and two women — were discovered on the *Endeavour*, apparently escapees from the Port Jackson penal settlement. (The two women were Elizabeth Heatherly and Ann Carey who were believed to be from the First Fleet transport ship *Charlotte*, which had arrived in Sydney in 1787. They subsequently became the first European women in New Zealand.)

Four of the stowaways were experienced carpenters and one of them, James Heatherly, husband of Elizabeth, was a shipwright. Their presence was to prove invaluable to their survival later.

The ships continued their voyage to Fiordland, but on 3 October struck very bad weather, and the *Endeavour* began to leak badly — so badly in fact that all hands were required to man the pumps continuously for days to keep the vessel afloat. By the time they reached Facile Harbour on 12 October a survey showed the ship was in such poor condition that the crew were surprised it had held together during the rough crossing, and it was condemned.

Captains Bampton and Dell rowed across to nearby Anchor Island to inspect the partly built schooner left by the 1793 sealers, and they found that while it had suffered some deterioration in the intervening years from sitting in the open, such as some of its timbers having shrunk and split, it was salvageable.

Not that they had a lot of choice. There were now about 244 people in Dusky Sound, far more than could be accommodated on the *Fancy*.

So they set about dismantling the *Endeavour* and shifting its supplies, ammunition and other equipment to the *Fancy*, while its masts, rigging and cables were taken ashore. At one point during this operation a raft they were using to get the goods ashore overturned, dumping two of the ship's cannons into the sea. There they remained until 1984 when they were recovered by the well-known Kiwi diver Kelly Tarlton. One is on display at the Southland Museum at Ōtatara in Invercargill and the other is in the Te Anau Museum.

On 25 October, the *Endeavour* was set adrift in the harbour and a couple of days later it drifted on the rocks where it remained. Today its resting site is marked by a pile of ballast stones made up of Sydney

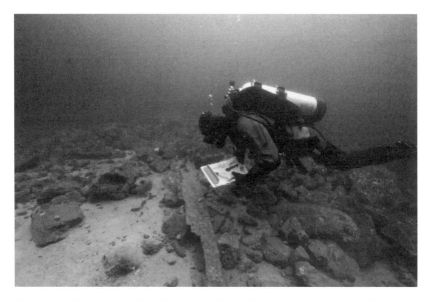

*Maritime archaeologist Dr Kurt Bennett catalogues the Sydney Brownstone ballast and wooden timbers remaining from the wreck of the* Endeavour *on the floor of Facile Harbour, Dusky Sound in 2020.*

Matt Carter, Toitū Otago Settlers Museum, Dunedin

sandstone, which is quite unlike the local rocks, and a few pieces of wood from the hull.

The castaways then turned their attention to the partly built schooner, which Captain Raven described as a small vessel with a 'forty feet six inch keel, thirty-five feet in length upon the deck, sixteen feet ten inches extreme breadth, and twelve feet hull'.

The vessel was planked and decked with 'spruce fir' (rimu) which he later reported the carpenters thought was inferior to English oak. However, he felt that it had been constructed with 'strength and neatness' which few shipwrights at the time would have been able to achieve in an isolated wilderness such as at Dusky Sound, and he was confident that, once completed, it would 'sail well'.

The four experienced stowaway carpenters, under the watchful eye and instruction of shipwright James Heatherly, along with some willing helpers, set to work to complete the partly built ship and eventually they were able to launch the vessel, which they named *Resource*, later changed to *Providence*. It was the first vessel built and launched in

New Zealand, and made entirely from local timber, in this case rimu.

However, their problems were far from over. *Endeavour* had been an 800-ton vessel, while the *Providence* weighed in at a mere 70 tons. The *Fancy* could accommodate 64 people and *Providence* 90, meaning they were short of space for some 90 people.

Their partial solution to that problem was to convert the *Endeavour*'s longboat for a voyage to Australia, which they did by stripping it back to its frame and recladding it with new timber and equipping it with sails, a task that took three weeks. When that work was completed, the rebuilt longboat was launched, and named *Assistance*.

However, *Assistance* could only accommodate 55 people, meaning 35 had to be left behind.

Captain Bampton himself took command of the *Fancy*, while its commander, Captain Dell, was placed in charge of the Dusky-built *Providence*.

With time and supplies running low, Bampton ordered the two ships to sea for the voyage to Bombay, via the Norfolk Island penal colony, and ordered the *Endeavour*'s First Officer, Waine, to take charge of rebuilding the longboat with instructions that when that was completed he was to sail to Sydney, leaving 35 men behind to look after their leftover supplies, who would be collected sometime later when it could be arranged.

*Fancy* and *Providence* departed on 7 January 1796, arriving at Norfolk Island on 19 January where Bampton unloaded 32 of the escaped convicts who had stowed away on the *Endeavour*, and alerted authorities to the fact that the *Assistance* was expected to arrive in Sydney early in February.

Bampton and the *Fancy* along with the *Providence*, now under the command of a Captain Murray, then sailed on to Bombay where he was in search of further cargoes. *Providence*, however, not being as fast as *Fancy*, was left behind, and finally made it to Batavia, now Jakarta, in what was then the Dutch East Indies. From there Murray and crew were repatriated to Sydney while the *Providence* remained at Batavia. What happened to the ship after that is unknown other than it is thought that it probably never left Batavia.

Meanwhile, work continued on rebuilding the longboat at Dusky Sound under shipwright James Heatherly, and *Assistance* with a complement of 55 passengers and crew under First Officer Waine eventually set off for Sydney where they arrived on 17 March 1796 in a 'miserable condition', after a hazardous crossing of the stormy Tasman Sea. They survived the voyage with no loss of life in what has been called a remarkable feat of seamanship because of the limited performance of the vessel and the desperate shortage of water and food aboard, as they had had to leave supplies behind for the castaways.

*Assistance* was later sold in Sydney but what ultimately became of the vessel is unknown.

Meanwhile the 35 castaways left behind at Dusky Sound struggled on in miserable and desperate conditions awaiting rescue. They survived on seals and fish and any birds they were able to catch.

Captain Bampton had undertaken that on reaching India he would send a ship to collect them and the surplus stores that had been left behind, but as time passed and there was no sign of a rescue, concern

*Sydney Brownstone ballast rocks from the* Endeavour, *on the floor of Facile Harbour, Dusky Sound in 2020.*

Dr Kurt Bennett

began to mount in Sydney. The end of 1796 came and went, still with no progress, and in March 1797, the Governor of Sydney decided that something had to be done to relieve the castaways. But that was easier said than done because for unknown reasons the Governor was unable to find anyone willing to undertake the rescue mission.

Finally, the captain of an American scow, the *Mercury*, agreed to the mission and the ship departed for Dusky Sound in the middle of May. Four months later in September of that year word reached Sydney that the castaways had been rescued and had been delivered safely to Norfolk Island.

Evidence of their presence remains at Dusky Sound today, beside the Sydney sandstone visible underwater where the *Endeavour* finally came to its sad end. The pile of rocks on which the *Providence* was built remains, the firepits where they operated their forge and steambox are still visible, but nothing remains of their house or storage hut, other than a pile of rocks where their fireplace stood.

# 1839

# THE WĀHINE WHALERS

In the early nineteenth century, the lure of whales and seals brought many Europeans to New Zealand.

By the nature of the industry, virtually all who came to these shores in search of the mammals were men — but there was at least one occasion where a whaleboat largely crewed by women was successful in capturing a whale.

European whalers and sealers first began arriving in New Zealand in 1808, when a sealing expedition from Port Jackson (Sydney), led by American Eber Bunker aboard the *Pegasus*, arrived at Whenua Hou Codfish Island — a small island about 3 kilometres to the west of Rakiura Stewart Island.

The first shore-based whaling station in the southern waters was established at Rakituma Preservation Inlet by Captain Peter Williams in 1828 or 1829, and that was followed by short-lived stations at Ōmaui, Waikawa, Fortrose and Bluff.

The most successful and the longest operating was a station opened at Jacobs River — now Riverton Aparima — by Captain John Howell, an entrepreneurial sailor, whaler, trader, pastoralist and later politician. He is remembered as one of the most influential and successful identities of early Southland, and a man closely involved with the wāhine whalers.

Howell was born in Sussex in 1810, and as a twelve-year-old was employed by a local farmer to shoot crows in his wheat field, for which he was paid threepence (2 cents) a week. About 1822 he and a companion, identified only by the surname Luxford, in search of excitement and adventure ran away to sea aboard a sailing ship bound for France. But on the return journey, to their surprise, the ship was impounded by Customs agents on charges of smuggling. The pair was locked up in jail until authorities concluded that, because of their age, they were innocents caught up in events beyond their understanding. They were set free.

Undeterred by that experience, Howell, this time with a second accomplice, William Portland, stowed away aboard a convict ship carrying prisoners to Australia. They were discovered when the ship was well on its way and brought before the captain who threatened them with a flogging, but again they were reprieved because of their age. Howell became cabin boy for one of the officers on the ship while Portland was put to work in the galley.

On arrival in Sydney, Portland went to work for a local cobbler, while Howell joined a whaling station at Two Fold Bay in southern New South Wales, remembered today for the role of orca (killer whales) in helping its whalers hunt baleen whales in the sea off the coast. The orca would find target whales, shepherd them into the bay and then swim to the area off the whaling station where they would alert the whalers by tail slapping. After the whales had been harpooned, the orca would often seize the ropes of the harpoons in their mouths and help the whalers haul their catch towards the shore.

As a reward, the whalers would anchor their catch near the shore and the orca would feast on the lips and tongues of the carcasses before they were hauled ashore for processing. Howell spent about five years at Two Fold Bay until 1827 or 1828 when he joined a whaling brig as first mate under Captain William Lovett, sailing to Kāpiti Island. But he eventually fell out with the brutal and bad-tempered Lovett and about 1833 moved south to join Sydney-born whaler and sealer Captain Johnnie Jones, a successful entrepreneur who at one stage owned controlling interests in virtually all South Island whaling stations, employing nearly 300 men. Over the next 30 years Jones became a significant landowner, organised settlement promoter, ship owner, trader, banker, newspaper publisher and pastoralist, and was an influential businessman and community leader in Southland and Otago.

Howell and Jones were similar characters and were alike in their temperament. They became firm friends.

Howell joined Jones at his whaling station at Waikouaiti and in 1834 was sent by Jones with three ships and 60 men to open a whaling station in Foveaux Strait to exploit the rich whaling resources of the area. After searching along the southern coast, in 1835 Howell settled on Jacobs River or Aparima as Māori knew it, as the site of the new station, which eventually employed 200 local Māori. The area was named after a heavily tattooed elderly Māori who lived in the area whom early sealers and whalers called Jacob.

*Captain John Howell.*
Te Hikoi Museum, Riverton
Aparima

At some point, probably around 1836, Howell purchased the Jacobs River whaling operation from Jones and became the sole owner.

A settlement was created with huts surrounded with gardens, and many of the men working at the station took Māori women for their wives. Generally peace prevailed but at the time, New Zealand was not a particularly peaceful place. The Treaty of Waitangi was still years away and in the North Island there was tension over land issues. In the South Island, Te Rauparaha had conquered the northern parts of the island, and had attacked Akaroa and Kaiapoi, slaughtering hundreds of people and with reports of widespread torture and cannibalism. There was general concern at the Jacobs River station at the prospect of attacks by Te Rauparaha or some of the local Māori tribes, including the Ngāti Māmoe — a Ngāi Tahu iwi — whose pā was based at Aparima.

An ally of Te Rauparaha, Te Pūoho of Ngāti Mutunga attempted an invasion of the area via Haast Pass in 1836, but his war party was intercepted near Mataura by Tūhawaiki, the leader of Ngāi Tahu in the southern South Island, which was known as Murihiku at the time.

While the Ngāti Māmoe appeared to have accepted the arrival of Pākehā among them, there was a degree of uncertainty and it was felt that Captain Howell needed to follow the example of his men and also take a Māori wife, thereby establishing a solid relationship between Pākehā and Māori.

By all accounts, Howell was an impressive figure. He was a tall, thickset, broad-shouldered man with extraordinarily long arms and large hands, and had bright blue eyes and curly fair hair. It is said that he respected and liked his Māori workers, admiring their skills as seamen and navigators.

While his fellow Pākehā were quick to take Māori wives, his hesitation to follow suit was creating tension with local Māori.

His Māori workforce obviously held him in high regard because of his respect for them and his fairness in dealing with them. It was made clear to him that if he were to take a Māori wife, he would enjoy great mana with the locals as a rangatira and would receive a large grant of land, the property of his wife, but he would have to remain among them. It was also made clear that by doing so, permanent peace would be established between his Pākehā workforce and local Māori.

It was decided that Howell should marry an eighteen-year-old Ngāti Māmoe chieftainess by the name of Kohi Kohi Patu, the daughter of the local hapū chief Horomona Patu, who lived on Rarotoka or Centre Island, a very small island about halfway between Riverton and Stewart Island.

It was said that she was very beautiful, and when told of her betrothal to Captain Howell, she was very happy with the decision.

On the morning of the wedding day, sometime in 1837, Kohi Kohi arrived at Howell's Point near Riverton from Rarotoka in a whaleboat festooned with ferns and native clematis and rowed by Māori whalers, and after landing on shore she was carried up to be presented to Howell by four Māori warriors.

Howell had not met or seen his wife-to-be and it is said that he was delighted with her and 'pleased at his good fortune'.

There was no British clergyman to perform the marriage ceremony, but history records that when Howell held out his hands and drew Kohi Kohi to him, the 'assembled congregation bore witness that he gladly accepted her as his spouse', and vice versa.

While celebrations went on into the evening, Howell and his new wife were aboard his ship catching the evening tide on their way to Sydney for their honeymoon.

Howell not only gained himself a wife but he also gained an enormous estate of flax- and bush-covered land stretching from Waimatuku south-east to Jacobs River as Kohi Kohi's dowry, which was the beginning of the large land holding he accumulated throughout his life. It is not quite clear what the dowry land was, because he also became the owner of some 50,000 acres (200 sq. km) of land north of Riverton, stretching from Fairfax to Wrey's Bush, also taking in Nightcaps, which was said to be the grant of land that Kohi Kohi had brought to him, or given to him as a gift 'by Kohi Kohi's people'.

On their return from Sydney they brought with them a supply of Australian gum timber which was used to build their four-roomed cottage in the Jacobs River settlement in 1837 or 1838, which was the

*Captain Howell's cottage, also known as Kohi Kohi Cottage, as it was in 2018. The cottage was built in 1837–38 and is one of the very few pre-1840 houses still standing. It was built of Australian hardwood and consisted of four rooms — two bedrooms, a kitchen and a parlour.*
Public domain, via Wikimedia Commons

first European-style house built there. The cottage is still standing and is one of the very few New Zealand buildings from before 1840 and is registered as a Category 1 heritage building.

They also brought with them horses and cattle for the farm they were to develop on the dowry land.

Howell and Kohi Kohi were now expecting their first child, and while the exact details of that event are a little uncertain, the fact of the wāhine whalers is quite clear and recorded.

Their first child, a boy they named George Robert Howell, was born in 1838 or 1839.

According to one report, the proud parents, wishing to show off their first-born to his maternal grandparents, set out for Rarotoka in a whaleboat with five Māori women on the oars. Also on the boat was Kohi Kohi's brother Horomona Patu, an experienced whaler, her personal servant, and an elderly Māori woman named Betsy.

Whaleboats were open, double-ended, clinker-built row boats usually about 9 metres long and were traditionally rowed with five oars and a steering oar.

Their voyage involved crossing about 10 kilometres of open sea, which was often rough with a strong swell, and they sang as they rowed their way across until one of the women spotted a large whale quite close to the shoreline and apparently unaware of their presence.

The women called on Howell to go after the whale, but Howell wouldn't because he was worried about having five inexperienced women on the oars. Horomona Patu was also against the idea, and both men urged the women to forget the whale and row on to their destination.

But the women weren't to be dissuaded and continued to pressure Howell to hunt the mammal until eventually Howell agreed, despite the risks he perceived because of his inexperienced crew.

One of the women took the steering oar from the captain, who then positioned himself in the bow with his harpoon and when the boat was alongside the unsuspecting beast, he plunged the harpoon into the whale, right into its heart.

They managed to avoid the danger of the dying whale's giant thrashing tail and body, and eventually secured their prize and set off back to Jacobs River. Nearing the bar at the Jacobs River mouth, their success was observed by the whale lookout located near the point now known as Howell's Point, and undoubtedly a large crowd would have assembled by the time they got their bounty to shore. Reportedly there was much rejoicing at the exploits of the women, and much appreciation of the bravery they had shown in capturing the whale.

The value of their catch was recorded at £500.

Another version of the story recounted in 1936 by the adult George Robert Howell, then aged about 98, was slightly different. He claimed that in fact he was born on that whaleboat when the entourage was returning from a visit to Kohi Kohi's parents on Centre Island, his birth occurring just before the sighting and capture of the whale.

George Howell lived in the family home in Napier Street until his death on 23 April 1937.

Captain Howell and Kohi Kohi had a second child, Sarah Ann, born in 1840, and Kohi Kohi died the following year at the age of 22 or 23. She was buried at her ancestral home on Centre Island. The two children were cared for by Betsy and Kohi Kohi's personal servant, whose name is lost to history, and then by Howell's half-sister, Ann Paulin, until 10 August 1845 when Howell married thirteen-year-old Caroline (Kararaina) Brown from Codfish Island. She was the daughter of Captain Robert Brown, a European who started a settlement at Codfish Island in 1823, and his Māori wife, Martha. Caroline was born on 23 September 1832.

She and Howell went on to have seventeen children together and they also fostered three orphaned children. She died in Riverton on 17 April 1899 at the age of 66.

In 1843 Howell had been joined at Jacobs River by his half-brothers George and William Stevens, and his half-sisters, Ann Paulin and Elizabeth Stevens, and Ann's husband and their infant daughter, who had all been living in the Hunter Valley in Australia. Ann and Elizabeth were the first European women in Southland.

Howell later took his half-brother, William, as a partner into the whaling business. But shortly after, realising that whaling was decreasing because the slaughter of whales meant their numbers were seriously declining, they set about diversifying their business interests to include farming, shipping, shipbuilding, food retailing, hotel ownership, sawmilling and trading. Whaling continued to decline until the late 1850s when the Jacobs River whaling station was closed.

In 1858 Jacobs River officially became Riverton and in 1998 was given the dual names of Riverton Aparima. In 1862 Howell was elected to the Southland Provincial Council, the year after the creation of Southland as a separate province from Otago which it remained until 1870 when the two were merged once again. He pushed strongly but unsuccessfully for Riverton to become the main port for the province and also advocated for a road link between the township and the Otago goldfields via Kingston.

In 1869, disillusioned at the decisions of the provincial council, he retired from political life and shifted his family to the huge Fairlight Station, another farming property he owned near Garston. Shortly after, his health began to decline and the family returned to Riverton once again to live in the second house the Howells had built in Palmerston Street.

In April 1874 Howell decided that a trip to Sydney might help his ailing heath, and he left from Bluff with his son Thomas aboard the steamer *Tararua* in April that year. But his health continued to deteriorate and eleven days after their arrival in Sydney he died on 25 May 1874 from stomach cancer. His body was brought back to Southland, arriving in Bluff on 28 June aboard the *Omeo*, and was conveyed by special train to Invercargill, and the following day was taken to Riverton also by train. He was interred in the Riverton Cemetery on Tuesday, 30 June 1874.

*A memorial to Captain John Howell was built in 1936 and unveiled in January 1937 as part of Riverton's centennial celebrations. The memorial sits at Howell's Memorial Park at the mouth of the Jacobs or Aparima River.*

Te Hikoi Museum, Riverton Aparima

# 1843

# NEW ZEALAND'S FIRST EXPORT BOOM

New Zealand and its economy boomed after Australian prospector Gabriel Read found gold in the bed of a Tuapeka River tributary near Lawrence in Central Otago on 30 May 1861.

It was to become the country's biggest gold strike, attracting thousands of prospectors from all over the world and helping to develop Dunedin into New Zealand's largest city at the time with a booming economy.

There were other gold finds: Tasmanian prospector Charles Ring found payable gold at Driving Creek near Coromandel town in 1852 and there were mostly short-lived rushes at Mōhua Golden Bay in 1856, Marlborough in 1862, the West Coast in 1865 and on the Coromandel again in 1865.

It has been said that almost 1000 tonnes of gold have been recovered in New Zealand, but no one knows for sure because of the way records have been kept and because of gaps and inconsistencies in figures.

But gold was not the first natural resource to be exploited in the early days of European settlement of New Zealand.

The first extracted material that lured ambitious men to the South

Island was nephrite jade, better known to us as greenstone or pounamu, a material so highly valued by the Chinese, who considered it to be an 'imperial gem', that it was more valuable than gold. Humans had been mining nephrite jade since about 3000 BCE, and in 1842, the Chinese were paying as much as £1500 per ton for greenstone.

(According to Wikipedia, nephrite is found in Europe, Canada, Australia and New Zealand, but New Zealand pounamu contains varying amounts of iron which gives it a wide range of shades, richness of green and translucency.)

It was realised in the early 1840s that a particularly good source of the material was Anita Bay, a remote bay on the southern entrance to Piopiotahi Milford Sound in South Westland.

In pre-European times Māori from Jacobs River (present-day Riverton Aparima) and nearby Pāhia travelled up the Waiau River to Lake Manapōuri and Lake Te Anau and from there made their way to the numerous pounamu fields including Anita Bay. Others possibly travelled to the area by canoe from settlements further north on the West Coast. In South Westland, pounamu was found in virtually all the rivers.

One of the first Europeans who attempted to cash in on the resource was the Irish-born whaler, Captain William Andrew Anglem, sometimes referred to as Anglin, Anglim or Hughlin.

Anglem is believed to have grown up in a monastery in Limerick and could apparently speak four languages, later adding te reo Māori to the list. He arrived in Van Diemen's Land as a crewman on the *Campbell Macquarie* about 1821, and by 1829 had risen to the position of ship's captain on the Bunn & Company whaling boat *Caroline* working out of Rakituma Preservation Inlet, the southernmost fiord in South Westland. A whaling station had been established there in 1828.

Later he joined the Port Jackson-based Weller Brothers who ran a whaling station at the Otago Harbour heads and who, in the late 1830s, became New Zealand's largest trader. He captained their whaling ship *Joseph Weller*, a 49-ton ship and the first built at Rakiura Stewart Island in 1831.

Later he captained another Weller Brothers ship, the *Lucy Ann*, and in 1834 was involved in protecting Europeans on the Otago Peninsula from marauding local Māori who were raiding ships and homes, setting fire to houses and threatening to kill the settlers.

Sometime in the early 1830s he married a Māori woman, Maria Te Anau, daughter of Te Wakaihua and Hinearohia, in Port Jackson (Sydney). There are varying accounts of their resulting family. Some sources say they had two children, others say three, and yet others say they had five children. Their first, a daughter, was born at Puysegur Point at the entrance to Preservation Inlet about 1830. By 1834 they were living at Port Jackson where their second child, another daughter, was born. Maria is recorded as being baptised there that same year.

In 1835 they were back in New Zealand, settled at The Neck on Stewart Island, a narrow peninsula that separates Paterson Inlet from Foveaux Strait, where there was a Māori settlement. From there, they supplied produce and meat to visiting whaling ships.

Their marriage and Anglem's association with her family probably played a significant part in his becoming involved in the greenstone industry, which was to have disastrous consequences for him.

As European settlement developed in Australia and New Zealand, so trade began to increase in the South Pacific. Ships bringing settlers, convicts and supplies to the Antipodes from the northern hemisphere obviously were looking for cargo for the return trip, and this led to the exploitation of the natural resources of the region by way of timber, sealskins, flax and eventually greenstone.

It seems that Anglem came up with the idea of exporting the stone, and he partnered with two entrepreneurial European settlers in Australia, Henry Elgar and Captain Ranulph Dacre, to pursue the enterprise.

Elgar had been involved in trading with China and was based in Canton or Macau and later moved to and lived in the Philippines. He arrived in Port Jackson in October 1840 and there he became involved in business deals with Dacre, who had been engaged in trading in New Zealand since the mid-1820s, mainly trees for ship's masts and spars. Dacre was a leading trader in Port Jackson at the time and even had his own wharf there.

According to one source, Anglem somehow met Dacre and Elgar at Port Jackson late in 1841 and told them that he had seen large blocks of greenstone at Milford Sound. The three of them put together a plan to mine the stone and ship it to China.

Anglem, Maria and Elgar left Port Jackson on 3 January 1842, aboard the *Anita*, a new 210-ton, 26-metre schooner apparently owned by Elgar, bound for New Zealand, arriving in Wellington on 19 January. They left again on 29 January claiming they were sailing to Manila, but in fact they sailed south towards Milford Sound.

On 13 April they arrived back at Wellington where they remained until 6 May, apparently with a cargo of Milford Sound pounamu aboard destined for the Chinese market.

The *Anita* wasn't the only ship they were using. While the other three were en route to New Zealand for the first cargo of pounamu, Dacre bought a second ship, the schooner *Royal Mail*, to join the fleet, which left Port Jackson for New Zealand sometime in January 1842. One report suggests that it was fitted out in preparation for its cargo of greenstone in Wellington before heading to Milford Sound, although there is no newspaper record of its arrival in Wellington at that time.

There is a record of it arriving in Wellington to join the *Anita* on 23 April 1842. It claimed that it had arrived there from Port Jackson via Auckland, but there is no record of it ever having been in Auckland.

Both ships sailed from Wellington on 6 May, reporting that they were heading for Manila in the Philippines, but it seems the *Royal Mail* instead headed to Stewart Island where Anglem picked up local Māori with knowledge of the pounamu sites and Māori workmen, before continuing on to Milford Sound. In September 1842 it was reported to be anchored in Milford Sound and 'engaged in collecting green stone for the China market'.

The *Royal Mail*'s first shipment was reportedly 10 tons of greenstone, valued at £15,000.

The *Royal Mail* arrived back at Port Jackson in October 1842 and left soon after for Nelson where another ship owned by Dacre, the 61-ton *Wave*, was berthed and together the two ships sailed for Milford Sound

*Harrison Cove where the* Royal Mail *and* Wave *sheltered while pounamu was mined from nearby secret locations. Photographed 2006.*
Wikimedia Commons

in November, mooring in Harrison Cove, about two-thirds of the way into Milford Sound.

Because of the general inaccessibility of the coastline and the wild seas in the area, the larger ships anchored in the shelter of Milford Sound while whaleboats were used to transport workmen and the greenstone between the shore and the ships.

They remained there for six weeks while workmen went back and forth in the whaleboats collecting the greenstone from a location that was a closely guarded secret. Whether they were loading the stone from Anita Bay, or some other locations, is unclear. There are reports of greenstone being recovered from Big Bay about 25 kilometres north of Milford Sound, and there are also reports of workmen being left at Barn Bay, 60 kilometres north of Milford Sound, to blast the rock and pack it into wooden cases for shipping, and this seems to have been their main source.

About two tons of the stone was loaded aboard the *Wave* in wooden cases bound with iron straps and in December the ship departed for Manila, stopping off at Nelson for supplies. The stone was finally delivered to Elgar who by then was back in Manila.

Anglem and the *Royal Mail* remained at Harrison Cove mining more greenstone, but trouble was just around the corner.

They were gathering stone, most likely from Barn Bay, but were having difficulty in breaking up the stone to manageable size, and they finally found the solution was to drill a hole into the rock and blast it apart with gunpowder.

But on 3 January 1843, there was an accident with the blasting which left Anglem with serious wounds to his hands and arms and damaged his eyes. Two other men were also injured in the mistimed blast.

Anglem's workmates bound up his eyes and put him in a whaleboat and set out for the *Royal Mail* in Harrison Cove, a journey that took them twelve hours. On 4 January, the *Royal Mail* set sail north to seek help, and ten days later they berthed at Nelson.

Primitive medical care during the voyage staved off the threat of gangrene in his injured limbs and when he was at last seen by a doctor on 15 January, he was suffering from badly injured hands, and one finger had to be amputated. He also lost the sight of one eye, as did one of the injured crewmen.

The *Anita* meanwhile arrived back in Wellington from Manila on 24 December, and on 14 January 1843, sailed for Milford Sound. It is likely that the *Royal Mail* crew left a message for them explaining their absence at a place known as Post Office rock, where ships' crews placed messages for each other inside bottles.

Anglem and the *Royal Mail* remained in Nelson until 15 February when it sailed again for Milford Sound, planning to join the *Anita*.

The two ships reportedly remained there until about May when, apparently laden with pounamu, they both sailed for Manila where they arrived in July 1843.

The *Anita* sailed on to China, but the Chinese were reportedly not happy with the quality of the greenstone. Some reports suggest the dealers didn't like the black specks and colour variations of the stone, while others suggest damage resulting from the use of explosives in recovering the stone made it unworkable by the Chinese craftsmen.

The result was that the shipment of greenstone went unsold, and it was eventually stored in a warehouse in Macau. There is a report that in 1851 a representative of Elgar paid the storage fees of some $US7000 and collected the 50 boxes of greenstone from the warehouse. But on 9 August 1852, Elgar died, apparently from a fever, on board a Chinese junk off the coast of Macau. He was 36. Thereafter the 50 boxes of New Zealand pounamu disappear from history and what happened to them is unknown.

The riches initially promised to the investors in the scheme never eventuated and in fact the whole exercise turned out to be a costly failure, with Dacre and Elgar both losing large amounts of money. Elgar's ship, the *Anita*, was put up for sale, and some reports suggest Dacre lost £10,000 in the process. Anglem came back from China penniless and settled again at the family home on Stewart Island.

*A fragment of nephrite recovered from Watson Bluff, just north of Barn Bay. Julia Bradshaw, Senior Curator of Human History at Canterbury Museum, has made a major study of pounamu exploitation in the 1840s. She believes this fragment was broken off by the use of explosives, illustrated by the fractures visible in the upper left side of the rock.*
Julia Bradshaw, Canterbury Museum

There is some evidence that he continued his involvement with ships and the sea, but little is known about his activities, other than that he suffered considerably because of the injuries incurred in the blasting accident. He died at his home on Stewart Island sometime in 1846, apparently after suffering a seizure while gardening. He was 46. Maria died in 1851 aged about 36.

Mt Anglem on Stewart Island was named after him by Captain John Lort Stokes of the *Acheron*. Stokes had used charts given to him by Anglem to help him map the coast of Southland, Stewart Island and Foveaux Strait. Stokes also employed Anglem as pilot for the survey.

Mt Anglem's Māori name is Hananui, meaning 'great glow', probably a reference to the sun's effect on the rocky peak early in the morning and later in the afternoon.

Over the following century and a half, there were other attempts to quarry the stone with varying success. But that came to end in 1997 when the government handed ownership rights of the stone to Ngāi Tahu, the principal tribe of the South Island.

# 1927

# AIRSHIP SERVICES PLANNED FOR NEW ZEALAND

In the 1920s there was much excitement over the possibility of international travel through the development of airships.

The plan was for New Zealand to be part of an international network with an airship mooring mast and associated equipment proposed on the site of the present-day Ōhakea Airbase in Manawatū.

The development of heavier-than-air flying machines had expanded tremendously during the First World War, and that had been matched by the development of airships — huge hydrogen-filled dirigibles that could cover vastly longer distances than the aeroplanes of the day. The landmark achievement of the time was the construction of the British-built airship R34 in 1919 which made the first east–west trans-Atlantic crossing from East Lothian in Scotland to Long Island in the USA. The trip took the 643-foot-long (196 m) aircraft four and a half days, and it arrived with just one hour's petrol left in its tanks. A few days later R34 left on the return flight, thereby making history's first return flight over the Atlantic.

It was the generally held belief at that time that airships would be used to cover long-distance routes, with aeroplanes providing feeder services on short-haul operations.

Great Britain recognised the opportunities that airships offered in terms of communications with its Empire, and at the Imperial Conference in London in 1921 agreed to set up a committee to investigate the idea of an Imperial Airship Company to operate airship services throughout the Empire, even as far as New Zealand.

The following year the British engineering company Vickers, in association with Shell Oil Company, put forward to the British Government a scheme to build a fleet of six huge airships to provide passenger services to the Empire. The idea was rejected but after years of political jockeying a revised version of the 1921 proposal was accepted and the Imperial Airship Scheme was launched.

The scheme proposed the construction of two new airships. The first, to be known as R100, would be built by a new Vickers company subsidiary, and the second, R101, would be built by the government-owned Royal Airship Works at Cardington in Bedfordshire, north of London. The plan was that R100 would utilise existing technology while R101 would be an experimental craft to try out new design ideas and new technologies. The two ships would be about 730 feet (222 m) long, contain five million cubic feet (141,550 cu. m) of hydrogen gas in sixteen separate bags, and would carry about 100 passengers and 10 tons of freight. There would be a 60-foot by 40-foot (18 m by 12 m) saloon, a dining room to seat 50, a dancing room, and they would have an unspecified number of two- and four-berth cabins. Smokers were to be given their own special room, obviously sealed and fireproofed because of the highly flammable hydrogen gas used to lift the ships.

Both craft would need to fly non-stop for 57 hours, cruising at 63 mph (101 km/h). They would be put to the test by flying from England to India with a refuelling stopover in Egypt. Later the final destination was changed from India to Canada.

It was intended that the service would operate throughout the Empire and to major world centres and would be run by a new organisation called Imperial Airways.

*This is R101, the second of what was to have been a fleet of airships serving the Empire.*
The National Archive UK via Wikimedia Commons

Under the original 1921 proposal the cost of the scheme was to be met by contributions from private enterprise, Dominion governments and the British Government, and six years later the 1927 Imperial Conference agreed that the Dominions would each be responsible for creating the necessary facilities for the proposed airship proving flights. That would require them to find suitable locations then erect mooring masts and build base facilities.

Officials of the British Air Ministry and the British Meteorological Office would visit each of the Dominions to advise on and assist with the establishment of these proving stations. On 29 August 1927, members of the British Airship Mission arrived in Auckland aboard the liner *Aorangi* from Sydney after completing their investigations in Australia, to begin the search for a suitable site for a mooring-mast and airship station for the proposed Empire Airship Service terminal.

The mission members were Group Captain P.F.M. Fellowes DSO, the Director of Airship Development and head of the Imperial Airways Commission, Flight Lieutenant S. Nixon of the Royal Airship Works and Mr Maurice Giblett, the Superintendent of the Royal Airship

Meteorological Division. The provision to airships of meteorological information on factors such as wind speed and direction, air pressure and weather forecasts along the route was critical to their operation. Such reports were required every six hours to enable airships to operate.

New Zealand had already appointed two men to look after its interests in the inquiry. These were Major T.M. Wilkes who was Director of Air Services for the proposal, and Captain J.L. Findlay who was employed as a pilot to provide air transport for the mission. A two-seater Bristol fighter biplane was provided so members of the mission could inspect potential sites from the air and move quickly around the country.

On 11 September 1927, Group Captain Fellowes made a presentation to MPs in Wellington, shortly before the team left New Zealand at the end of its mission.

Fellowes explained that it was planned to make the first airship trial flight in 1928 from Britain to Cape Town in South Africa using R100, followed by trials of the Britain–Egypt–India service. The trial of the service to New Zealand was expected to take place with a demonstration flight in 1930 and regular weekly scheduled services were expected to begin in 1935. A fleet of 20 airships was envisioned at a total cost of around £5 million.

The cost of R100 was quoted at £275,000 and it was expected to cruise at about 100 mph (160 km/h) non-stop for 4000 miles (6500 km) when loaded at full capacity, flying at a height of 2500 to 3000 feet (762 m to 914 m). Estimates were that R100 could fly passengers and mail from Britain to New Zealand in eleven to fourteen days, about a third of the time taken by ocean liners. Fares for the scheduled service were expected to be about 25 per cent higher than steamer salon fares.

Fellowes told MPs that mooring towers were already being built for the airships in England, Malaya, India, Canada and South Africa.

A suitable base for the New Zealand end of the service would need to be at a location with generally good weather conditions, as near as possible to sea level (height above sea level reduced the freight-lifting capacity of airships), have a ready supply of fresh water for ballast, and

*R101 being hauled to the mooring mast at Cardington RAF Base, Bedfordshire, England, in 1929. This was the type of mast that would have been erected at Ōhakea had the project gone ahead. Passengers would enter the airship through this tower, and walk through the interior of the giant balloon body to reach the passenger accommodation area. It was from here that R101 departed on its fatal final flight on 4 October 1930.*
Airship Heritage Trust, UK, www.airshipsonline.com

be at least 10 miles from hills or mountains to avoid troublesome air currents which made landing the airships difficult.

After checking several possible sites in both islands, the mission presented its report to the government in 1928, recommending Ōhakea as the most suitable site. The estimated cost of building the 200-foot-high (61 m) mooring mast and associated equipment, including a gas-generating plant for the proving flight, was about £200,000.

The plan was to eventually build a complete airship base which would have meant three mooring masts, huge airship storage sheds and a hydrogen gas generating plant.

The development of a Britain–New Zealand airship service depended on whether the Australian Government decided to participate in the grand scheme, because the New Zealand service was an extension of the Britain–Australia service.

Initially the New Zealand Government put the decision on joining the scheme on hold pending the Australian decision, while the Australian

*An unusual shot of the underbelly of R.101 in 1929 showing both sets of promenade deck windows, dining room, and bedroom/staterooms corridor, on both sides of the ship. R101 was 774 feet (237 m) long.*

Airship Heritage Trust, UK, www.airshipsonline.com

Government decided to delay a decision because of uncertainties about the viability of the proposed service and the costs involved. It also decided to wait and see the outcome of a proposed trans-Atlantic service which was scheduled to begin later in 1928.

In March 1928 the Australian Government opted not to join the proposed proving flights, delaying any further commitment until there was 'further and better evidence of the utility of giant gasbags'.

In Britain meanwhile, plans were going ahead for the construction of two more even larger airships, to be known as R102 and R103.

The plan was for scheduled monthly services to Canada and India, and weekly services to Egypt with a service to Australia and New Zealand starting in 1936 with a proposed R104, an even larger airship.

There was not unanimous support for the concept of the huge airships among British politicians and the public, and concerns about the whole enterprise were realised on 5 October 1930, with the crash of the airship R101 south-east of Beauvais in France on its proving flight to India.

The airship nose-dived to earth, crashed and burst into flames, killing 48 of the 54 people aboard, including Lord Thomson, the Air Minister who had initiated the programme, and most of the airship designers from the Royal Airship Workshop. R101 was flying with a hastily organised Certificate of Airworthiness, the haste apparently being the desire of airship proponents to complete the proving flight to India before the conclusion of the 1930 Imperial Conference, at which future funding and support for the airship programme was to be considered. The cause of the crash was never established.

Its sister ship, R100, which had a relatively trouble-free history, including a successful trans-Atlantic return flight to Canada in July and August of 1930, was grounded immediately and its gasbags deflated. The following November it was put up for sale as scrap, eventually selling for a mere £600.

The crash of R101 ended the British Government's experiments with airships for international travel, with Cabinet formally abandoning the scheme on 31 August 1931.

However, the R101 crash wasn't the end of airship disasters. The final blow came on 6 May 1937, with the horrific destruction of the German airship, *Hindenburg*, at Lakehurst, New Jersey, when it exploded in flames, killing 35 people on board — 22 crew and 13 passengers — but with 62 survivors.

It's thought that static electricity discharging as the airship moored to its tower and igniting free hydrogen gas was the cause of the disaster. Later there were rumours that the ship had been sabotaged, but these claims went unproven.

The *Hindenburg* disaster was captured by a newsreel cameraman and, along with a recorded radio eyewitness report of the disaster, made for dramatic and shocking coverage that was seen in movie theatres around the world. The disaster completely destroyed faith in the concept of airships and brought the era to a close.

The work of Group Captain Fellowes and his mission members in New Zealand was not wasted, however, because in 1935 the new Labour Government undertook a plan to expand New Zealand's military air capabilities, and Ōhakea was chosen for a major development as an airbase. By 1939 and the outbreak of the Second World War, two hangars had been built ready for use and during the war Ōhakea became the main training base for aircrew.

# Firsts

# 1901

# SPEEDING CAR NARROWLY AVOIDS SERIOUS ACCIDENT

Christchurch motorist Nicholas Oates was the first motorist in New Zealand to be charged with speeding after driving down the city's Lincoln Road at speed, and very nearly 'causing a serious accident'. Businessman Oates was driving into the city, probably to the office, showroom and factory of his bicycle manufacturing and sales business at 82 Manchester Street on the morning of 1 May 1901, when the near serious accident occurred.

At the time Oates owned the bicycle manufacturing company, Zealandia Cycle Works, with his business partner Alexander Lowry. It was the first cycle manufacturing business in New Zealand and had been established by Oates in Christchurch in 1880. Lowry had been a retail manager with menswear manufacturer Hallenstein Brothers, and joined Oates in 1897 to form Oates, Lowry & Company.

It was a very successful business in a booming market and became the largest manufacturer of bicycles in New Zealand and Australia with branches in Timaru, Ashburton, Wellington and Napier.

It had two successful brands of cycles, Zealandia and Atalanta, and ran with a staff of about 40 people. It was a modern manufacturing facility and utilised the latest technology including an 8 horsepower Tangye steam engine and a complete electric-lighting plant.

Oates was clearly someone who appreciated and adopted new technology. In 1891 he imported the first pneumatic-tyred bicycles and tricycles into Christchurch, so it's not surprising that the advent of the internal combustion engine and self-propelled vehicles caught his attention.

In 1899 he went to England and Europe to investigate this new development and the problems of the bicycle industry. It had been through a period of enormous growth resulting in over-investment in manufacturing and it was facing collapse.

The advent of the internal combustion engine had also changed the dynamics of personal travel, and overseas bicycle manufacturers were increasingly turning to the newly developed engine and its application to vehicles.

Oates visited a number of car manufacturers during his trip and travelled extensively around England in the new invention, and he was so impressed with his experience that he purchased a three-seater vehicle to bring back to Christchurch.

Oates reported that 'great things' were expected of the motor car in England where it had become a popular means of conveyance, but it was Paris in particular that impressed him.

'Here everything in the streets gives way to the motor car, even the trams pulling up to let it pass,' he told a local newspaper on his return. 'It fairly takes charge of the city, and the drivers, who are extremely reckless, rush hither and thither at a breakneck pace. The pace is such that one needs to hold on to his hat all the time.'

The modern reputation of Parisian drivers is nothing new apparently. Oates said he 'was much struck' with the reckless driving of the Parisians.

'The cabs and omnibuses appeared to dash all over the place,' he reported. 'The drivers keep up a constant shouting, and the din, to a stranger, who does not understand a word of the language, is worse than Bedlam.'

*Charles Nicholas Oates (right) and his 1895 Benz Velo motor car photographed in Christchurch in June 1901. With him are two of his children. His other passenger is identified as a Mr Denton.*

Photo from *The Canterbury Times*, June 1901. Christchurch City Libraries

He purchased his car, an 1895 Benz Velo (short for Velocipede) at the Paris Exposition in 1899 and brought it to Christchurch in October 1900 to become the first motor car in the South Island. The three-seater car was one of only 134 built and cost him £250 ($500). It came with solid rubber tyres, a 3-horsepower single-cylinder engine, and a belt and chain transmission. It had a guaranteed top speed of 16 mph (25 km/h), or 17 mph (27 km/h) in favourable winds. The cars were built by Carl Benz, who held the world's first patent for the internal combustion engine, and it was the world's first large-scale production car.

In November 1900 Oates made the remarkable trip from Christchurch to Timaru, which took him two days with an overnight stop in Ashburton. On the 29th he travelled around the streets of

Timaru, the car attracting a great deal of attention from locals. He even took a reporter from *The Timaru Herald* for a ride, who recorded his impressions in the newspaper the next day:

> *What did strike us about it, was the immense improvement that would be made in the cleanliness of the town if all vehicles were horseless. It is driven by a tiny gas engine, the gas being a light oil called petroline, vaporised by the heat from the engine exhaust, and ignited by electric sparks supplied by a small storage battery. Horses took little or no notice of the car. The one defect noticeable in a first ride is the vibration caused by the engine, which shakes the car with every explosion. The wheels have solid rubber tyres; two inches wide pneumatic tyres are often used — but Mr Oates doubts their safety. The wheels are of small diameter, and this brings out prominently the unevenness of the streets.*

While the horses of Timaru took little notice of the noise of the Benz Velo, Christchurch horses it seems weren't so unfazed, and it was this that resulted in Nicholas Oates becoming the first person in New Zealand to face a charge of speeding.

He was charged with driving a motor car within the city at a speed greater than 4 mph as prescribed by the city bylaws.

Oates was driving the Velo along Lincoln Road towards the city when he noticed a horse-drawn carriage stopped outside Christchurch Hospital. He told the Christchurch Magistrates Court that as he approached, he noticed the horse was restless, but that the groom gave him no indication that he should stop, so he sped up a little to pass them, coming to a stop in nearby Antigua Street.

The carriage was owned by a George Gould, and his groom told the court that he was waiting outside the hospital when he 'saw the car approaching from the Addington direction at a speed of 10 to 12 miles an hour. The horse took fright and immediately bolted,' he claimed, and he had the greatest difficulty in controlling it, and not before the carriage had 'suffered considerable injury' when it collided with a City Council dray.

The groom told the court that the horse was 'not a restive animal' and could be made to go past a traction engine. He said the motor car went past at such a speed that he was unable to see how many people were in it.

Other witnesses told the court that the motor car went past at a speed of at least 10 mph and that a serious accident was only averted by the prompt and skilled actions of the groom in handling the horse. One witness, a Dr Nedwell, told the court that he never saw a man manage a horse better than the groom did in the emergency.

In his defence, Oates told the court that the car was fitted with two gears, and the maximum speed obtainable with each was 14 mph and 6 mph. He had been driving using the high-speed gear while coming into town but changed to the lower gear at the corner of Lincoln Road and Tuam Street. He was positive that he had not gone faster than 7 mph while passing the carriage, but he did admit to travelling along Lincoln Road itself at 13 mph. He said he had slowed the car down to 5 mph before he saw the horse, but admitted that he did speed up 'perhaps to seven miles an hour, at most, to pass it' when he saw the animal was restive.

He told the court that that was the safest way to pass an animal which was likely to shy, and that was 'always used with motor cars at home' (meaning England).

The magistrate convicted him and fined him 20 shillings ($2.00) plus court costs.

But that wasn't the end of the matter.

Two months later, Oates was before the court again, this time being sued by the owner of the horse and carriage, George Gould, who was seeking £23 in damages as a result of the incident — £3 ($6) for damage to the carriage, and £20 ($40) for injuries sustained by the horse.

Gould told the court that 'one of the animal's legs had been very sore afterwards, its temper and nerves had been spoiled by the fright, and that its character was gone'. As a result, he claimed the market value of the horse had fallen from £40 to £20.

The court gave judgement for the plaintiff but decided that a total of £15 ($30) was sufficient compensation for him.

Oates was back in court on driving charges again in November 1922, this time on a charge of driving a motor vehicle between stationary trams and the kerb, for which he was fined 40 shillings ($4.00) plus costs.

Nicholas Oates appears to have been something of an unscrupulous character despite his business success.

In 1904 his wife, Catherine, petitioned for a judicial separation from him on the grounds of cruelty which she claimed was injuring her health. She told the court that she and Oates had had ten children of whom six had survived. She claimed he had not supported her or the children financially, had had a series of affairs with other women, had hit her in the face with a shoe and verbally abused her, and had sent the children to boarding school and not allowed her to see them. At one point their youngest daughter had had an operation but Oates hadn't told his wife about it, and she was unable to find any details about the operation or to see the child.

A host of witnesses supported her claims, including Oates' own son and daughter, and Mrs Oates' doctor who opined that his patient's circumstances would 'injuriously affect her health'. The judge declared that Oates' own evidence had 'made a much more conclusive case for his wife than she had herself', and that he had not the slightest hesitation in holding that the wife was justified in seeking separation. He granted the decree, with the matter of alimony to be decided later.

Oates died at his home in Bordesley Street, Linwood on 5 April 1938 at the age of 85.

The Benz was sold to a new owner in Ashburton, but there it was involved in an accident in which a pedestrian was knocked down in what the *Ashburton Guardian* described at the time as 'an atrocity'. It was onsold to a Thomas Kilworth of Creek Road, Ashburton who in turn passed in on to his son, Edwin. He often drove it to Methven or to Christchurch with the family aboard. The trip to the city usually took about three hours at a steady 12 mph (19 km/h).

Later he dismantled the vehicle and used the engine to power his lathe until about 1928 when the cylinder cracked in a heavy frost.

# 1905

# BUMPY HISTORY OF STATE HOUSING

The opening of the first state house at 12 Fife Lane, Miramar in Wellington, by the first Labour Government Prime Minister, Michael Savage, on 18 September 1937, is often seen as a turning point for New Zealand society.

But that wasn't the first time the New Zealand Government had stepped in to build housing for the population. The first state houses in fact were built in 1906 under the Workers' Dwelling Act which had been passed by the Liberal Government the previous year.

At the time urban housing for the working class was slum-like, with poor quality buildings, overcrowding and without amenities such as rubbish removal, sewerage and fresh water.

Under the 1905 scheme, the plan was for 5000 well-built homes for families who were earning less than £156 ($312) a year.

The houses were built in Auckland, Wellington, Christchurch and Dunedin between 1906 and 1910, with the first built in the Wellington suburb of Petone. After 1910, the scheme was extended to provincial centres including Palmerston North, Napier, Whanganui, Greymouth, Ashburton, Waimate and Ōamaru.

Under the 1905 scheme, there were three options for the occupants: they could rent the houses weekly, lease them for a period of 50 years with a right of renewal, or they could lease the property with the right to buy with payment spread over a period of 25 to 41 years.

Under the Act, women were as equally entitled to a house as a man, but in fact that was discouraged because of fears that it might lead to the establishment of 'houses of ill-repute'.

In Christchurch, by June 1913, there were 51 occupied houses under the scheme, with seven more opening in 1914.

The promoter of the Workers' Dwelling Act was the Liberal Party Premier Richard ('King Dick') Seddon. His plan was for the houses to be architecturally designed and not planned to a set format, so each house would be individual. Local architects were asked to submit ideas for the houses in their towns through design competitions.

They were to have six rooms — a kitchen/ dining room, a lounge, three bedrooms and a bathroom, and were to cost no more than £300 ($600), a figure later increased to £400 ($800). The annual rent of each property was to be 5 per cent of the capital cost of land and buildings, plus rates and insurance. That meant weekly rents from 10 shillings and sixpence ($1.05) to 12 shillings and seven pence ($1.26).

Seddon was responsible for many innovative policies besides the Workers' Dwelling Act, including old-age pensions, women's suffrage, tenure reform and labour arbitration, ideas that earned New Zealand a reputation as 'the social laboratory of the world'. In fact, they were part of the modernisation of the country as it moved towards Dominion

*Liberal Party premier, Richard Seddon saw many benefits from the state building housing for workers.*

Muir & Moodie, Public domain, via Wikimedia Commons

status in 1907. The Workers' Dwelling Act meant that the New Zealand Government was the first in the world to provide housing for its citizens.

Seddon believed the Act would help stamp out slum living conditions and would increase the income of workers by making housing more affordable. He also believed that providing reasonably priced accommodation would help to drive down housing costs.

The first 25 houses were built in Petone in 1906, but circumstance meant that the occupants were no better off than they would have been if they had lived in central Wellington and paid higher rents. To get to their jobs in the city meant a 20-minute walk to the train station at Petone, then a 30-minute train ride into Wellington at a cost of 2 shillings (20 cents) a week.

The result was that only four families applied for the Petone houses, forcing the government to raise the maximum income limit and offer weekly tenancies to finally fill them. The same problem arose with houses built at Belleknowes in Dunedin.

*One of New Zealand's first state houses, built at 6 Patrick Street, Petone, under the Liberal Government's 1905 Workers' Dwelling Act. This property was designed by Hurst, Seager & Wood of Christchurch, and was constructed in 1906. This photograph was taken in 1913 and is believed to show the owner, accountant Percy Jewett, and his wife, with their young daughter at the gate and family dog.*
Ref: APG-0448-1/2-G, Alexander Turnbull Library, Wellington, New Zealand

Other houses built under the scheme, such as the eight in Sydenham (Christchurch), twelve at Newtown (Wellington) and twelve at Ellerslie (Auckland), were snapped up because they were close to the factories and shops where people worked.

Seddon died in 1906 and that same year the Advances to Workers Act was passed, which made cheap finance available to anyone looking to buy or build a home. The Act allowed for the advance of up to three-quarters of the value of the house and land, and a maximum of £350 ($700), paid back over 36.5 years at an annual interest of 5 per cent.

By 1910, only 126 houses had been built under the 1905 Act. The 1906 Advances to Workers Act still enabled people to rent or lease their homes from the government, but also introduced a scheme under which a homeless family could build a home with just a £10 ($20) deposit, with the government funding the balance. Under this scheme, anyone applying for a loan would pick the design of the house they wanted from the 24 plans approved by the Labour Department (later reduced to fifteen plans). It was a huge success, with 1296 loans approved by 1910.

Seddon's plan to build 5000 state houses fell well short. The Liberal Party remained in office until the 1912 election when the Reform Party and William Massey took power. It continued with Seddon's scheme until wartime shortages brought about its demise in 1917, by which time only 640 houses had been built. After 1917, the Reform Government began to sell off the houses.

But by 1919, the housing shortage was at crisis point again with large numbers of demobilised soldiers looking for housing, along with shortages of both raw materials and skilled tradespeople, which resulted in long delays in construction and big increases in building costs.

As well as selling off its state houses, the Reform Government took action to promote private ownership of housing through loans from the State Advances Office. Its Housing Act set up a Housing Branch within the Labour Department and a Housing Board to purchase existing houses and build new ones. It also reduced the income threshold for eligibility for state loans and made money available to local authorities to buy land and build new housing for workers.

The Department moved quickly and bought a block of land in Miramar, Wellington that provided 70 sections. Contracts were awarded to local builders to construct the houses, which became known as 'Massey Houses'. The plan was to build them in concrete because of the shortage of raw materials arising from the First World War, although some were in wood. To save costs, all had virtually the same interior, but changes were made to the outside appearance to avoid them all looking the same.

Rentals for these Miramar houses were set at 27 shillings a week ($2.70).

Under this scheme almost 650 houses were built, but the scheme itself became embroiled in controversy over costs and construction methods. As a result, in 1921 the government declared the building target had been met and closed the Housing branch of the Labour Department. Instead, it set up a State Advances Department to provide housing loans to people wanting to build or buy their own homes, which Prime Minister Massey believed would bring more votes for his Reform Party.

In the 1930s, following the Great Depression, housing was once again at crisis point in New Zealand. Many homeowners had lost their homes because they couldn't afford the mortgage repayments. Meanwhile the population was increasing sharply, and once again there was a severe housing shortage. That ultimately led to the Labour Government's iconic state housing scheme of 1936.

There were many factors involved in the creation of the 1905 and 1919 Housing Acts, but probably the biggest was politics: the 1905 Workers' Dwelling Act was the work of the Liberal Party with its liberal social reform policies, whereas the 1919 Housing Act was from the Reform Party which favoured freehold tenure and state home loans so people could build their own homes rather have the state build them.

Some aspects of both schemes, such as the practice of scattering state-built homes throughout the suburbs rather than in large-scale areas of state housing, and the use of tenders for private builders to build the homes, were carried over into the Labour Government's state housing scheme.

Initially the 1935 Labour Government had no plans for building state houses, favouring providing low-cost loans to people to build their own homes instead. That was why it nationalised the Mortgage Corporation of New Zealand, renaming it the State Advances Corporation of New Zealand. The Mortgage Corporation had been set up in 1934 by the Coalition Government to provide low-interest housing loans after the Great Depression.

But Labour realised that even with low-cost loans, there was not enough housing being built and in 1936 it had a change of heart, with Finance Minister Walter Nash announcing a plan to build 5000 rental state houses. It proposed that the houses would be built by private enterprise, with a new Department of Housing Construction set up to manage the construction, and with the State Advances Corporation managing the houses.

As the government saw it, its plan would not only provide badly needed housing but would also provide employment in construction and manufacturing — and it did.

Just over three years later the target had been met with 5000 new houses built, mainly in the Hutt Valley, Miramar and Ōrākei, Auckland. The peak was reached in the 1990s when the government owned 70,000 rental properties.

# Human Nature

# 1869

# IMMORALITY AND OUR EARLY SETTLERS

Maintaining a high level of public morality and preventing such social evils as prostitution occupied much of the public discourse in nineteenth-century New Zealand.

There was concern throughout the country at the widespread incidence of venereal disease, and the feeling was that if prostitution could be controlled the spread of associated contagious diseases such as syphilis and gonorrhoea could also be controlled.

There was also a widely held belief that legislation to control contagious venereal diseases was the best way to also control the 'growing social evil' of prostitution, which was increasing in New Zealand.

By the 1860s prostitution and the spread of venereal diseases were becoming serious issues. There was also a more practical reason for the concerns, and that was the effect the diseases were having on men in the British Army and the Royal Navy, who made up a substantial proportion of the male population of New Zealand.

Prostitution itself was not a crime but soliciting, living off the proceeds of prostitution, keeping a disorderly house and vagrancy were all illegal and were used to detain women working as prostitutes.

Concerns over prostitution in New Zealand started with the visit of Captain James Cook in 1769 and grew from there. That visit also introduced venereal diseases to the Māori population. Cook was disapproving of his crewmen having sex with native women of the islands they visited, aware that they would spread venereal diseases, but he was unable to prevent it.

He wrote in his journal: 'A connection with Women, I allow because I cannot prevent it, but [I am] never encouraging.' Inevitably, early sailors, whalers, seal hunters and traders visiting our shores were regularly exchanging European treasures such as muskets, iron goods and alcohol for sex with Māori women, and from the early days of Europeans arriving here a booming sex industry developed.

The immigrant population of New Zealand in the early nineteenth century was mainly male. Their numbers increased with the arrival of British troops and sailors after fighting broke out between Māori and Europeans in the 1840s and continued to increase until 1865 when there were 10,000 Imperial troops in the country. In 1864 the New Zealand Government adopted a policy of 'self-reliance' with settlers and 'friendly Māori' taking over the fighting. In 1866 British forces began to be withdrawn, with the last contingent, the 18th Regiment, leaving in February 1870.

The discovery of gold in 1852 also meant a huge increase in single men coming here. That was inevitably followed by the establishment of hundreds of hotels on the goldfields which often employed women. These gold rushes also attracted women working as prostitutes.

With the influx of large numbers of young men and the shortage of marriageable young women, entrepreneurial settlers saw the potential profitability of making sexual services available. The resulting increase in the number of prostitutes and the associated increase in prostitution led to a heightened sense of propriety among many of the church-based settlements, particularly in the South Island, which led to increasing social pressure on police and politicians to take action to control what was seen as a social evil.

One report said there were ten 'working girls' in Christchurch in 1864, but that had jumped to 39 by 1867.

*In Christchurch in 1858, women made up only about a third of the adult population. Assisted immigration for suitable young women resulted in some 12,000 single working-class women arriving in New Zealand between 1860 and 1880, such as this unidentified young housemaid in her white apron and cap uniform cleaning a Christchurch house. The sudden influx of women caused a panic among the elite of Christchurch and Dunedin who saw them as a threat to the morality of society.*

Photograph by Peter Schourup, about 1880. Photograph owned by Miss Ruby Victoria Jackson. Ref: PA2-2083, Alexander Turnbull Library, Wellington, New Zealand

The influx of goldminers and soldiers in the 1850s and 1860s meant New Zealand had a huge population imbalance. In Christchurch in 1858, women made up only about a third of the adult population. Pressure was mounting on provincial governments and on immigration organisers to bring in more eligible single women who would also be able to undertake domestic work.

Provincial governments set about trying to correct the imbalance through assisted immigration for suitable young women, and between 1860 and 1880 some 12,000 single working-class women arrived in New Zealand. The plan was to provide society with female domestic workers while helping to address the population imbalance.

However, the sudden influx of young single women caused a panic among the elite of Christchurch and Dunedin who saw them, and the demand for prostitutes, as a threat to the morality of society.

The impact of venereal disease on members of Britain's armed forces was of real concern because of the effect on military vitality and the availability of manpower in the army and navy. A new Navy Station was about to be opened in Auckland and there was concern among government officials at the effect venereal disease might have on sailors at the new establishment.

Earlier attempts to control prostitution had made provincial governments responsible for the control of brothels in their districts, and some introduced by-laws banning them altogether. One of the first attempts, the 1866 Vagrancy Act, provided for imprisonment for up to three months — sometimes with hard labour — for women deemed to be behaving in a 'riotous or indecent manner'.

In Christchurch in November 1867, concerns reached such a level that a public meeting was called to discuss 'the causes and remedies for prostitution in Christchurch' and specifically to:

- Examine existing means of repressing prostitution
- Recommend ways in which to 'bring this evil under the better control of the law and police'
- Consider the establishment of a permanent society for the prevention of vice
- Consider ways 'for the reformation of fallen women'.

The meeting formed a committee to consider these issues which reported to another public meeting in February 1868, chaired by the Dean of Christchurch, The Very Reverend Henry Jacobs. The committee recommended legislation to the General Assembly which would 'give larger powers for the suppression of the evil'.

Things moved quickly, and later that year the General Assembly set up a Select Committee on the Social Evil to consider the issues, which were identified as:

- The extent to which venereal disease of both classes exists in the Colony, and the advisability of legislation to prevent its spreading, and secondly
- The necessity of providing for the control of houses of ill-fame, and the prevention of annoyance to the community from want of proper power of supervision by the police.

*The Very Reverend Henry Jacobs, headmaster of Christ's College (1850–63), Sub-Warden of Christ's College (1850–97) and Dean of Christchurch who chaired a public meeting in 1868 that called on the government for 'larger powers for the suppression of evil'.*

Sewell Journal, Wikimedia Commons

In August 1869, the Committee put a Bill before the General Assembly which was aimed at controlling prostitution and preventing contagious diseases.

In introducing the Bill, the independent MP for Avon (Christchurch) William Rolleston said it was of a 'double character — the control by the police of the evil in question and the maintenance of public decency'. The Bill was largely a copy of British legislation — the Act for the Better Prevention of Contagious Diseases — which Rolleston said had been found to work 'exceedingly well in England in the garrison towns'. Rolleston told the Assembly that it was difficult to ascertain the number of cases of venereal disease because many sufferers didn't consult with medical practitioners, but rather treated themselves or were treated 'by quacks or chemists'. But what evidence there was suggested the numbers were high.

Cases of syphilis had doubled in four years while the incidence of other venereal diseases had increased fourfold.

Dunedin Hospital had treated 90 cases of venereal disease over the previous two years, while 26 cases had been treated at Dunedin gaol. In the same period there were 56 cases at Christchurch Hospital and nine cases at Christchurch gaol, while in Auckland there had been 44 cases in 1868 alone.

Rolleston said the diseases were rife in the towns, but country areas weren't immune, with cases existing 'among the labourers and shepherds up-country'. The Act was known as An Act for the Better Prevention of Contagious Diseases — or The Contagious Diseases Act 1869 for short — and was passed by the General Assembly and signed into law on 3 September 1869. It largely emulated the British Act of the same title enacted in 1866.

It allowed police to detain women deemed to be 'common prostitutes' and subject them to genital examination, detention and medical treatment. Modern critics point out that while the Act made no reference to race it was clearly aimed at white working-class women whose actions had largely precipitated its creation.

Its effect was rather limp. The Act required provincial governments to ask the General Assembly to declare the Act operational in their regions, and it seems that only two did so — Canterbury in 1872 and Auckland in 1882.

In Christchurch a special section was built at Addington Prison known as the Addington Lock Hospital, in which women were detained if they were found to have an infection. But that only lasted until 1885 when it was closed, while Auckland revoked the law in 1886 after four years in effect. Conviction rates under the Act were very low. In fourteen years, there were just under 200 convictions under the Act while the more widely applied Vagrancy Act accounted for 3000 women convicted of prostitution offences.

While the introduction of legislation like the Act for Better Prevention of Contagious Diseases might have satisfied some on the moral right, there was general disquiet about it and other similarly intended legislation. Many felt that they degraded women, violated their individual rights, failed to reduce the transmission of diseases, failed to eradicate prostitution and, worst of all, enabled a double standard because they imposed restrictions and enforced physical examination of infected women but did not impose the same requirements on infected males.

The British Parliament enacted contagious disease laws in 1864, 1866 and 1869, and opposition to them began in Britain as early as 1869. Opposition to the similar laws in New Zealand began with a campaign in 1882 to repeal the Act for Better Prevention of Contagious Diseases, but it wasn't until after New Zealand women won the right to vote in 1893 that opposition really began.

Widespread protests from women's groups, religious groups and others took place over the years from 1882 until the Act was finally repealed in 1910. But it took time — between 1895 and 1903, there were seven attempts to repeal the legislation, all of which were stymied by opposition in the Legislative Council.

Eight years after the repeal of the Act there followed a worldwide epidemic of venereal disease, with infections brought back to New Zealand by soldiers returning from the First World War. It has been estimated that within the New Zealand contingent serving overseas in that conflict, there was always at least one battalion out of action because of venereal disease.

In the 1919 epidemic, treatment clinics were set up in Auckland, Wellington, Christchurch and Dunedin and they were quickly overwhelmed with cases.

Increasingly, the problems of venereal disease occupied the minds of politicians, health professionals and social welfare groups to find an answer to the issue, which was once again seen as a menace to the social and moral welfare of New Zealand and New Zealanders.

It reached such a pitch that in 1923, the government set up a Commission of Enquiry into Venereal Diseases, which largely placed the blame on 'the prevalence of promiscuity, alcohol, the lack of sex education, loose women, amateur prostitutes and feeble-minded females'. Controversially, the Committee also recommended legalised prostitution and the use of prophylactics, two recommendations that were soundly denounced on moral and health grounds.

Until penicillin was developed during the Second World War, there was little that could be done to treat venereal diseases. Before then, people infected were sometimes not aware of it, and often did not seek treatment because of the stigma associated with the infections, which were usually seen as evidence of immorality and degenerate behaviour.

Sexually transmitted diseases were present among the populations of antiquity and are recorded in the writings of ancient Greek, Roman, Chinese and Indian physicians, and in the Bible's Old Testament. Even in those early times, they were usually seen as divine punishment for promiscuous behaviour.

Syphilis was first identified and recorded in Naples in 1494. Left untreated it causes madness, paralysis and death. Babies born to infected mothers are often deformed, or pregnancy ends in miscarriage.

Gonorrhoea was first recognised in the fourteenth century in the Parisian district formerly known as Le Clapiers — perhaps the source of the slang expression 'the clap' for venereal diseases. Untreated it causes urinary infections, genital discharge and fevers, while babies born to infected mothers are usually blind. Gonorrhoea often becomes dormant after a few years of infection.

From the eighteenth to the early twentieth centuries, infections were treated with mercury, arsenic and sulphur, which in themselves often led to serious side effects or even the death of the patient.

The first effective treatment for syphilis was the drug arsphenamine, also known by the trade name Salvarsan, which was introduced in 1910. The next advance came in 1939 with the use of the drug sulphapyridine as a treatment of gonorrhoea. But it wasn't until the development of penicillin in 1943 that these diseases became easily curable.

# 1893

# EDITOR'S LESSON: DON'T MESS WITH THE BURLESQUE GIRLS

Theatre entertainment in nineteenth-century New Zealand tended to be somewhat proper and certainly a lot less daring and explicit than we've become used to over the last 50 years.

So, when the London Gaiety Burlesque Company toured New Zealand in 1893 with a series of stage shows that were rather bawdy by Victorian standards, it caused some controversy in some parts of society, particularly in Dunedin where the show was performing at the Princess Theatre in High Street. A column in a local weekly newspaper — *The Otago Worker* — attacked the show, suggesting 'scandalous behaviour' by some of the young women involved, comments that led to the editor being horse-whipped and his newspaper office wrecked.

Precisely what owner and editor, Samuel Lister, writing under the pseudonym 'The Chiseller', said about the young ladies is not clear, other than his comments had 'cast aspersions upon their character' by

*The opulent auditorium of Dunedin's Princess Theatre as it was in 1893. This was the second theatre on the site replacing the first that burnt down in 1876. This view from the dress circle towards the stage, with its traditional proscenium arch, was featured in the* Illustrated New Zealand Herald, *in August 1876. The theatre was demolished in 1958.*

Hocken Collections — Uare Taoka o Hākena, University of Otago

suggesting the performers were paid so badly that they must have been forced to resort to prostitution to survive.

Obviously the young women were unhappy at the suggestion — so unhappy in fact that on 5 June 1893, they chose a deputation armed with horsewhips and — backed by their management, their male counterparts and stage hands — headed to the newspaper's office in Kensington to remonstrate with the editor and demand an apology and retraction.

Williamson and Musgrove's London Gaiety Company had been performing to packed houses in Dunedin as part of a seven-week-long New Zealand-wide tour with shows such as 'Miss Esmeralda', 'Faust Up to Date' and 'Carmen Up to Date', the latter two based on the operas Faust and Carmen.

The 90-strong cast and crew had arrived in Dunedin aboard the steamship *Rotorua* on 27 May, and their performances opened that same evening to a rapturous reception from the sold-out house. The performances of the leading ladies of the shows, and consistent crowd favourites — Addie Conyers, Alice Lethbridge and Alice Leamar — brought standing ovations every night. Special trains were put on from Ōamaru and Invercargill, to allow locals to attend the shows.

The shows were the first of their kind seen in the colony and by all accounts, everyone was delighted by the performances, apart it seems from Samuel Lister. After the publication of the allegations, the actors

*Addie Conyers. Newspaper critics described her performance as 'strikingly successful', saying 'as a vocalist her rendering of Within the Maze of Love's Sweet Dream was charmingly tasteful and sympathetic.' This led to demands from the audience for an encore 'to which Miss Conyers acceded.'*

New York Public Library, Digital Collection

*Alice Lethbridge. One reviewer wrote that Alice Lethbridge danced most gracefully and acted with much ability. 'Miss Lethbridge contributed three gracefully executed dances, to two of which she granted encores – declining, however, to repeat the third, which was of the hornpipe order and much more trying than the others. The dance in question was excellently given, and the applause which it evoked was loud and continuous.'*

Public domain, via Wikimedia Commons

*Alice Leamar also won the approval of the reviewers and the audience, with one reviewer writing that she 'obtained the lion's share of encores with one for each of two dances, one for her singing of Madame Duvan and another for Twiggez-vous.' Another reviewer commented: 'Those who saw the lively way in which Miss Alice Leamar danced Ta-ra-ra-boom-de-ay . . . could have no idea that this young lady was suffering from an aching heart, caused by the receipt a few hours before the performance began of cable intelligence of the loss of a favourite sister. Nothing but a strong desire to keep faith with those who had gone to witness the performance would have induced Miss Leamar to fulfil her contract with the public on that evening,' he wrote.*

Public domain, via Wikimedia Commons

met with Williamson and Musgrove management with everyone agreeing that the comments couldn't go unchallenged, and failing a published apology, the editor should be horsewhipped.

Two days later with no apology forthcoming the cast met again and according to contemporary reports, 'six of the most stalwart ladies of the chorus were picked out to represent the whole number in seeking satisfaction for the aspersions that had been cast upon their characters'. Then armed with 'property' horse whips they marched to the offices of the newspaper in south Dunedin.

Three of the company's management — H. Musgrove, W. Hughes (the Business Manager) and E.J. Lonnen — went in first to talk to the editor and demand a printed apology, which Lister was not willing to concede, whereupon the ladies of the chorus 'who had been deputed to vindicate the honour of those who had been maligned' entered the office 'in dramatic style' and on identifying the offender, promptly attacked him and began to 'lash their whips vigorously about his head and shoulders'. At this point Lister's two sons, John and Alexander, and the newspaper's compositors came to his aid. The attacking actresses were driven back by the newspaper's staff, but then the attackers called in reinforcements in the form of some of the stagehands who had been waiting outside, at which point a full-scale brawl broke out in the office.

According to newspaper reports at the time,

> . . .the whole of the premises were turned upside down and every window in the place was smashed in the conflict. While the free fight was proceeding between the stagehands and the compositors, the ladies re-entered and made havoc of the office — tearing up manuscripts and throwing documents about with a most sublime disregard for their literary value.
>
> The one of the defending force who fared worst was in the act of flight when he was intercepted by a couple of the attacking party, who smeared his face so that he resembled an Australian blackfellow.

Having wrought sufficient havoc to satisfy their wounded feelings, the attackers were withdrawing and about to return to the theatre, when the local policeman — Constable Higgins — appeared on the scene and was quickly enlightened of the attack by Lister. He urged him to arrest three of the attackers who he said had caused most of the damage and assaulted him.

Constable Higgins arrested the three men and took them to the Dunedin police station where formal charges were laid against them. That didn't satisfy Lister, however, because he believed the whole theatrical company had been involved and he demanded that charges be laid against them all, finally identifying 14 others involved who were arrested and charged. In total ten men and eight women were charged in connection with the attack.

An *Otago Daily Times* newspaper reporter on the scene at the police station appeared to be enjoying the spectacle, pointing out that large numbers of the public gathered outside the station to watch proceedings and they were sharing the good-hearted and humorous mood of the accused.

> *While the officer whose duty it was to record the charges against the accused was busily engaged in taking down their names and making out the several charges against them, they beguiled the time with talking jovially over their recent exploit, their conversation being enlivened with merry laughter and frequent jest. It seemed indeed as if a picnic party had paid a surprise visit to the police station and were jocularly pretending to be implicated in some offence against the law. What further gave their visit to the station the appearance of a picnic was the fact that at frequent intervals members of the Gaiety Company who were not under arrest appeared on the scene with refreshments which were demolished by the party in custody with evident zeal.*

When the police had completed their processes, the accused were driven away from the police station to the police court, *not in the customary dingey vehicles in which accused are generally conveyed to the Police Court, but in carriages drawn by high-stepping steeds. It seemed as if they were riding in triumph to some joyful event — the reward for their past victory — rather than to the awful precincts of the police court.*

Even in the courtroom, their high spirits were undiminished, and they 'appeared as excited and jubilant as players who had achieved a success before a large audience'. And they did indeed have a large audience, because a huge crowd of spectators had gathered in the courtroom to watch proceedings. They were charged before three Justices of the Peace with wilfully and maliciously damaging property of the value of £10 at Kensington, belonging to Samuel Lister, and with assaulting Samuel Lister and his two sons.

But the case came to an end when, apparently with the agreement of Samuel Lister, the prosecutor asked for the charges to be dismissed, which the defence agreed to and to which the police presented no objection. When the charges were withdrawn, and the offenders discharged, they 'shook hands cordially with the police, thanked them for their courtesy and withdrew, still jubilant, from the precincts of the court'. Contemporary reports say public sympathy lay with the Gaiety Burlesque Company, which continued to enjoy full houses for the rest of its week-long season in Dunedin.

# 1911

# NATIONAL SPARROW-SHOOTING CHAMPION FOUND

There was a time when New Zealanders enthusiastically took to the English sport of sparrow shooting, and in the later nineteenth century and until the middle of the twentieth century, sparrow-shooting clubs and competitions were commonplace throughout the country. The first sparrow shooting national championship took place in Christchurch on 6 July 1911.

Sparrows were first introduced to New Zealand in 1859 by homesick British settlers, and in the hope of reducing crop insect pests.

But as with so many introduced foreign species, they quickly became more of a pest than those they were supposed to control, which led to many varied methods of trying to eradicate them.

The house sparrow, or English sparrow, with the species name of *Passer domesticus*, has a long and strong association with humans. At various stages it has been seen as a pet, used as a food source, and sometimes seen as a symbol of lust, of sexual potency or vulgarity.

Just who organised the initial release of the birds in New Zealand is lost to history, but it is believed that fewer than 100 birds were initially involved.

There was much excitement in 1859 when a Canterbury man, identified as Mr Brodie, announced that he was bringing 360 sparrows to Lyttelton aboard the sailing ship *Swordfish*. He proudly proclaimed that the birds had been 'carefully selected from the best hedgerows in England'. Brodie claimed that the need for the birds was 'admitted on all sides to keep down the grubs. There is no security in this country against the invasion of armies of caterpillars taking off the grain crops as clean as if mowed by a scythe', he said. Unfortunately for Brodie, by the time *Swordfish* arrived in New Zealand, all the birds had died.

After that, there was a major effort, often by local acclimatisation societies, to introduce exotic species to the colony.

During the 1860s, hundreds of sparrows, along with other exotic species, were brought into the country, and some people even set up breeding operations here to meet the demand. Enthusiastic settlers handed over significant sums of money to purchase them.

In December 1867 the sailing ship *Water Nymph* discharged a cargo of English birds in Auckland which had been imported by the Auckland Acclimatisation Society. The birds were sold at a public auction that

*In 1862 one of these sparrows cost homesick immigrants 11 shillings ($1.10), the equivalent of two days' pay for a labourer at the time.*
Dr Phil Battley, Asst Professor in Zoology, School of Natural Sciences, Massey University, Palmerston North

attracted widespread interest from settlers, who bought them with the intention of releasing them in their gardens.

Eight of the sparrows in the shipment were bought for 11 shillings ($1.10) each and seven were bought for 9 shillings (90 cents) each by Mr T.B. Hill of Freemans Bay; eight went to T. and S. Morrin of Ōtāhuhu for 10 shillings ($1) each; and seven were bought by S. Jones of the city for 10 shillings each.

A Mr Claude of Papatoetoe bought eight partridges from the shipment for a total of £8-15-0 ($17.50).

By way of comparison, a labourer's wages in 1860 were about 5 shillings (50 cents) per day, while a skilled tradesperson was paid about 10 shillings ($1) a day. Eighteen months later, in May 1869, the Auckland Acclimatisation Society imported a shipment of sparrows and thrushes, along with a consignment of monkeys aboard the brig *Waverley*. What became of the monkeys is unknown.

In retrospect, the lists of foreign species brought into the country were frightening. In July 1869, *The Lyttelton Times* published a report of the activities of the Otago Acclimatisation Society which shows that during 1867 and 1868 it was responsible for releasing the following species in the Otago province:

- 3 hares
- 4 fallow deer
- 4 black swans
- 3 white swans
- 18 pheasants
- 3 Australia quail
- 51 blackbirds
- 49 finches
- 31 starlings
- 35 larks
- 18 hedge sparrows
- 33 chaffinches
- 42 goldfinches
- 8 greenfinches

- 18 linnets
- 10 redpolls
- 8 yellowhammers
- 14 house sparrows
- 2 mountain sparrows
- 26 Australian magpies
- 2 Australian plover
- 2 Australian landrails
- 6 Australian bronze-wing pigeons
- 54 song thrushes
- 4 skylarks
- 18 California quail
- 5 Java doves
- 2 laughing jackass (laughing kookaburra)
- 5 bush kangaroos
- 28 English perch
- 18 tench (freshwater fish)
- English oysters
- Australian frogs
- 400 trout

Many people — including the officialdom of the day — believed that introducing sparrows would solve the problem of insects destroying wheat, oat and barley crops. But what wasn't generally understood at that time was that sparrows are predominately grain-eaters. They feed caterpillars and insects to their fledglings but as adults, grain, seeds and ripe fruit make up the majority of their diet.

The species flourished in New Zealand and their numbers grew very rapidly, probably because of their ability to rear three or four broods a year, the lack of predators, the ready supply of food and the benign climate. The English naturalist Thomas Kirk calculated in 1878 that one pair of sparrows could theoretically lead to a population of 322,000 in five years.

Just a few years after the enthusiastic release of the birds it became clear that sparrows were becoming a major pest in the country.

In New Zealand, as had occurred overseas, it was soon realised that rather than feeding on crop- and fruit-destroying insects, sparrows preferred the crops and fruit themselves, with the result that fields and orchards were stripped bare, leading to large losses and calls for their eradication.

Settlers in the United States and Australia, where sparrows and other English birds had been introduced, were also facing the same issues, as were farmers and fruit growers in Britain and on the Continent. That led to the introduction of many schemes to eliminate them. They included widespread poisoning and the introduction of bounties for sparrow eggs and heads, which became a popular and profitable pastime for youths in the latter half of the nineteenth and early twentieth centuries.

In 1874, the Ellesmere Road Board in Canterbury spent the princely sum of £93 ($186) on efforts to control sparrow numbers in its district by the use of poison, which it subsequently declared a failure.

Local farmer John Mill complained at the plan to eradicate sparrows in the district, claiming he had lost more grain to caterpillars and insects in one year than he would lose to birds in 50 years. He thought it would be impossible to grow crops in Canterbury without the aid of the birds to clean up the pests.

By early 1875, the sparrow problem had reached such proportions in New Zealand that some of the acclimatisation societies were beginning to take action to try to control the sparrows that they had introduced less than ten years earlier.

The Canterbury Society asked the Provincial Superintendent to issue a proclamation permitting anyone to shoot sparrows, and in 1880 it was proclaimed legal for anyone to kill sparrows and linnets (finches) anywhere in the colony.

In 1881 farmers in the Springston district of Canterbury unsuccessfully petitioned Parliament to abolish all acclimatisation societies and to redirect all the associations' fees and licences to local bodies 'to be expended in undoing the injury said to have been inflicted on the farming community by the importation of sparrows and such birds'. That same year the government set up a Sparrow Commission to look into the problem, which recommended the eradication of sparrows and the introduction of bounties on sparrow eggs and heads.

The fight against the birds in Canterbury and Otago was launched with a vengeance. In the summer of 1883–84, the Temuka Road Board paid out bounties on 10,394 dozen sparrow eggs and young birds, the Geraldine Board paid out for 5492 dozen and the Levels Board paid for some 10,000 dozen. That means that more than 316,000 sparrows or sparrow eggs were destroyed in the area, along with a large number killed by poison that were not accounted for.

By 1894, the problems that had been created by importing foreign species were widely recognised, so much so that the Southland Acclimatisation Society dispatched a deputation to Wellington to protest at plans by the Canterbury Acclimatisation Society to import English wood pigeons. The deputation spoke of the 'evils resulting from the introduction of sparrows and other birds' and wanted the government to take control of the importing of exotic species.

The Colonial Treasurer, who received the deputation on behalf of the government, agreed that no foreign bird or animal should be brought to the colony until the approval of a competent authority had been obtained, and he promised quick action by the government to give 'careful attention' to the matter.

In Europe and in the USA large-scale sparrow eradication schemes had been introduced with limited success.

Attempts were made here, as had happened overseas, to poison the sparrows using strychnine, and bounties were introduced on sparrow heads and eggs. The bounty paid on eggs was threepence (2 cents) per 100. Sparrow poisoning clubs sprang up in many parts of the country and in 1880 it was reported that Cantabrians had poisoned thousands of the birds. There was also a demand for live birds which could be used in the growing sport of sparrow shooting. In this, live sparrows were placed in traps and released singly for competitive shooters to try to kill.

Sparrow shooting sprang to prominence in England in the 1820s and 1830s after changes were made to game-hunting laws which had placed restrictions on shooting rights.

Pigeon shooting had become a pastime for the rich which resulted in the poorer working classes turning to cheaper pursuits. Pub owners were quick to catch on to the opportunities and often organised handicap and sweepstake shooting matches with sparrows as targets, which offered more challenging shoots than the larger pigeons. Starlings were also often used as targets.

Sparrow and starling shooting clubs spread widely throughout England in the nineteenth century, a pastime that was brought to New Zealand and other colonies by emigrants and was encouraged as a means of reducing sparrow numbers.

Sparrow shooting clubs were quickly established throughout New Zealand and Australia and in both countries regular club and regional competitions were held to find the champion sparrow shooters. These events were often held weekly, regularly attracting 20 to 30 shooters. Many local shooting clubs held their own sparrow shooting championships.

Obtaining the birds could be a problem on occasions. In 1879 the Taitapu Sparrow Club secretary reported that he had bought 14,938 sparrow and linnet eggs for 11/2 ($1.12) a dozen and had managed to purchase 3046 birds at threepence (2 cents) a dozen.

Shooters used shotguns and were awarded so many points for a kill with the first barrel, with lesser points for having to use the second barrel.

The Amberley Gun Club held its local championship competition in August 1911 and a newspaper report of the times noted that 'the birds were a fast and tricky lot and not one of the thirteen competitors managed to kill the allotted number of twelve from the 20-yard mark', although two of them did manage to 'grass' eleven birds each. The previous year's champion, L. Stackhouse, only managed to grass ten birds.

The first New Zealand sparrow-shooting championship was held at the Spreydon Gun Club in Christchurch in July 1911.

Weather on the day was fine with little wind, and according to newspaper reports at the time the shooting was 'of a very high order'. Of the 31 competitors entered, 29 qualified for the finals. Shooters had three rounds of seven shots each, one at 18 yards, a second at 20 yards and the third and final at 23 yards. To qualify for the final round, they needed to score a total of ten kills from the first two rounds.

Two of the competitors, Allan Fraser and T. Preece, killed all their birds (21), and had to shoot off for the championship title and medal. In that round Fraser killed another 20, making his tally for the day 41 sparrows out of a possible 41. Preece missed one bird in the final, scoring 19 for the round, for a total of 40 out of 41. The two men decided to split the prize money, taking home £23-14-0 ($47.40) each. But as the inaugural New Zealand champion, Fraser took home the gold medal.

The New Zealand championships continued every year until at least July 1937 when it was won by D.P. North of Whangārei.

As well as the New Zealand national sparrow-shooting championship, there were also championship matches for both the North and South Islands and regional and club competitions. However, these had largely ceased by the late 1930s, when sparrow shooting was losing its appeal. There were moves by the Federation of New Zealand Societies for the Prevention of Cruelty to Animals and other animal welfare groups for it to be banned, along with pigeon-shooting competitions.

In England the sport came to an end in 1921 when laws were introduced banning live bird shooting. Evidence produced before the British Parliament showed that in 1920 alone, one million starlings and half a million sparrows had been killed in these competitions. The victims of the competitions were usually sold off for food, with sparrows being the more popular. Apparently they were very good for making puddings.

Australia also banned live bird shooting in the early 1920s.

In New Zealand things moved a little slower. A private members bill, the Captive Birds Shooting Prohibition Bill, was introduced to the Legislative Council in 1925 by G.M. Thomson, the MP for Dunedin North, but did not go ahead because the House of Representatives adjourned before it could deal with it. The Bill was a replica of the 1921 English legislation.

Thomson said the shooting of captive birds was a relic of the barbaric ages and had survived longer in New Zealand than it had in most other countries.

The Bill was introduced to the Legislative Council on six occasions but failed to reach the House of Representatives each time. Some MPs supported the Bill, believing the practice was cruel, but others opposed it because they saw it as an additional way to rid the country of sparrows.

The Federation of New Zealand Societies for the Prevention of

Cruelty to Animals tried in 1934, and again in 1937, to have legislation introduced to prevent the shooting of sparrows and other birds in organised competitions.

It tried again in August 1938 with its proposed Protection of Birds Bill but was unable to have the bill introduced to the House, when the Minister of Internal Affairs, W.E. Parry, refused to take it forward.

The president of the Federation, Clyde Carr, who was also an MP, told members at the 1938 Federation conference in Wellington that the government was opposed to any government MP introducing private members bills which 'might arouse opposition'.

In the end there was no need for legislation to stop the sport. In the 1930s public interest in the sport was fading and by the end of that decade, it had disappeared altogether.

*Clyde Carr, president of the Federation of New Zealand Societies for the Prevention of Cruelty to Animals, and the long-term Labour MP for Timaru.*

Public domain, via Wikimedia Commons

# 1914

# PRETTY ACTRESS COSTS GOVERNMENT PILOT HIS JOB

New Zealand's first 'government pilot', Captain Joe Hammond, brought about an early end to his appointment when on 28 January 1914 he flew a government-owned Blériot aeroplane over Auckland with a young actress as his passenger.

Hammond's flight, taking an actress from a visiting theatrical company rather than a male dignitary, incensed New Zealand's military leaders and politicians who immediately fired him and grounded the aircraft, eventually returning it to England.

Joseph Joel Hammond was born in Bulls on 19 July 1886. Some sources cite his birthplace as Gonville, others Feilding, others Palmerston North and yet others Marton.

He grew up on the family farm at Rangitīkei and was educated at Palmerston North's Campbell Street School on the corner of Main and Princess Street, and later became a boarder at St Patrick's College in Kilbirnie, Wellington.

Hammond was obviously an adventurer: he completed his education in 1901 at the age of fifteen and probably worked on the family farm until 1904 when he left for Australia where he worked on a sheep station for a brief period before travelling to Hawaii and later to the Klondike in Canada where he mined for gold. This proved unprofitable so he turned to trapping in Alaska then in 1905 he moved to Phoenix, Arizona where he worked as a cowboy on a cattle ranch. He returned to New Zealand for a holiday at the end of 1905. Five months later he was back in North America and joined Buffalo Bill's Wild West Show, which later became Buffalo Bill's Wild West and Pawnee Bill's Great Far East Show, more commonly known as the Two Bills Show.

He stayed with that troupe until 1908 when he moved on to Europe and England, basing himself in Seaford in East Sussex where he met and in 1909 married Ethelwyn Wilkinson.

The couple moved to France where Hammond was able to take flying lessons with the pioneering aviator Ferdinand Léon Delagrange who had taken up flying in 1907 and who was at the time ranked as one of the top aviators in the world. He was killed at Bordeaux when the wings of his Blériot XI collapsed as he was preparing for an attempt on the world distance record. Hammond also had lessons with the renowned Henri Molla at the Sanchez-Besa school at Mourmelon.

He gained his pilot's licence — a French Aviator's Certificate (No. 258) — in October 1910, becoming the first New Zealander to obtain a flying certificate. The following month he also obtained a Royal Aero Club Aviator's Certificate in England.

He then joined the British and Colonial Aeroplane Company as a demonstration pilot and salesman. The company made the Bristol Boxkite aircraft, a 'pusher'-type biplane and one of the first aeroplanes to be built in any quantity.

Hammond and his wife, and two Boxkites (aircraft numbers 10 and 11) were sent to Australia by the company to demonstrate the aircraft, in the hope of selling some to the Australian Government, a trip that was to produce many aviation firsts.

The entourage arrived in Western Australia in December 1910, and Hammond took off on the first of seven flights he made in aircraft Number 10 in the state in January 1911. It was the first aircraft flight in Western Australia.

The Boxkite was then dismantled and shipped to Melbourne where it subsequently made the first aeroplane flight in Victoria. Hammond also made the first cross-country flight in Australia (from Altona to Geelong and back), made the first passenger flight in the country (with one of his mechanics), took the first woman to fly in Australia (his wife), made the first charter flight carrying a passenger (a local businessman), who was also the first Australian to take flight, and also flew with two passengers aboard, the nation's first multiple passenger flight.

Altogether they made 40 flights in Melbourne before moving on to Sydney where he made the first-ever flight in New South Wales.

As part of the effort to appeal to the military he took several defence department leaders for flights, including one flight from Sydney to a training camp at Liverpool.

The Boxkite clearly demonstrated the outstanding performance of the design, flying further, higher, with heavier loads and with better control than anything seen before.

By the end of the trip in May 1911, aircraft Number 10 had made 72 flights in Australia, flying more than 1200 kilometres. It was then dismantled for the voyage back to England. The other aircraft, Number 11, still in its packing case, was sold to an Australian dentist who subsequently became the first Australian to gain an Aviator's Certificate.

Hammond and his wife didn't go back to England with the rest of the party. They sailed to New Zealand for a short holiday and so that Hammond's family and friends could meet the new Mrs Hammond. But while he was here, he was hit with a series of health issues, beginning with appendicitis, then pneumonia and finally blood poisoning, and the couple didn't return to England until May 1912.

Hammond continued with the British and Colonial Aeroplane Company until August that year when he joined the Eastbourne Aviation Company's flight training school. In February 1913 he switched employment again, this time to the Royal Flying Corps Military Wing as a Second Lieutenant.

Meanwhile, other developments were happening which were to lead to his return to New Zealand and his eventual sacking by the New Zealand Government.

With a very unstable political atmosphere in Europe, in May 1913 the Imperial Air Fleet Committee presented the New Zealand Government with a Blériot XI-2 two-seater monoplane, an aircraft that had gained lasting fame after making the first crossing of the English Channel in 1909. The Blériot XI-2 was named *Britannia* and was dismantled for shipping to New Zealand where it arrived in Wellington in September, albeit without its propellor which was still back in England. The machine was temporarily stored in Wellington's Cook Street Barracks waiting for the vital propellor.

The New Zealand Government hired Hammond to fly the machine and he arrived in Wellington in November 1913. He told a *Dominion* reporter that the Blériot was 'the best type of machine extant', and that it was the one favoured by the majority of independent pilots.

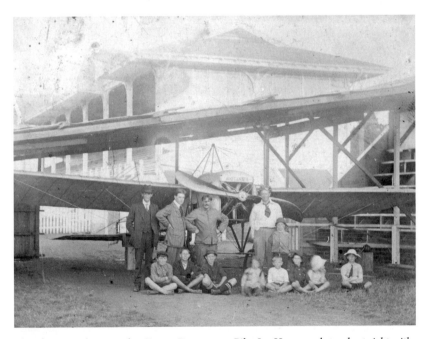

*The Blériot on the ground at Epsom Racecourse. Pilot Joe Hammond stands at right with goggles.*
Air Force Museum of New Zealand, Wigram, Christchurch

*Britannia* sat in the Barracks for three months, during which time Hammond gave it a thorough overhaul while he waited for the propellor to arrive, which it did on 27 December. He volunteered to fly the Blériot to Auckland, an offer rejected by defence authorities worried about the possibilities of it crashing on the way. Instead, it was dismantled and loaded onto a train and taken to Auckland, where it was reassembled and made its first flight in New Zealand from the Domain on 18 January 1914.

Hammond made a number of test flights in the Blériot over the next few days, in preparation for a public exhibition scheduled for Auckland's Anniversary Day, 29 January. In between those test flights, the Blériot was put on display at the Auckland Industrial, Agricultural and Mining Exhibition at the showgrounds.

*The Blériot XI known as Britannia, airborne at Epsom Racecourse, January 1914.*
Air Force Museum of New Zealand, Wigram, Christchurch

But fate was to intervene in the grand plan for Anniversary Day in the form of a young Australian actress who was staying in the same hotel as Hammond.

Esmee McLennan was from Brungle in New South Wales and was educated at the Goulburn Convent of Mercy where she excelled in music. That talent led to her joining Stanley McKay's Royal Pantomime Company where she was a celebrated soubrette, that is an actress who specialises in lively, flirtatious roles. The company was in New Zealand as part of an Australasian tour of the pantomime *Old Mother Hubbard*, in which Esmee was cast as Hafiz. One reviewer said she 'looked particularly nice' and described her performance as 'bewitching'.

Hammond and McLennan must have met and talked at their hotel, and it seems there must have been some attraction between them. McLennan, discovering that Hammond was an aviator — and a very famous one at that — suggested to him that if he ever felt like taking a passenger on a flight, she would be willing.

On 28 January, McLennan and other members of the cast visited the Industrial, Agricultural and Mining Exhibition at the showgrounds where Hammond was also present. He had already made one test flight, and he — apparently on the spur of the moment — offered to take McLennan for a flight, an invitation which she readily accepted.

At 6 p.m., the Blériot took to the skies with her aboard for a 20-minute jaunt over the city, taking in the Waitematā Harbour and the city itself, reaching a height of 2000 feet and travelling at speeds of up to 80 miles an hour (130 km/hr). McLennan later described it as:

> We were travelling faster than I have ever travelled in the fastest express trains, but there was not even the slightest vibration, nor was there any sensation that was other than entirely pleasant. When we can actually journey from one place to another without the fatigue of train travelling or the drawbacks of a sea voyage, how delightful it is going to be.

To commemorate the experience, during an interval of her performance on stage that night Hammond presented her with a bouquet of flowers, and the cap and goggles she had worn for the flight.

She might have been thrilled with her flight, but New Zealand officialdom was certainly not impressed, and the fallout was instant.

The Defence Department immediately forbade Hammond from flying again, and the planned flights over Auckland were cancelled.

The contract that Hammond had with the government had been terminated on 12 January for unknown reasons, after which he had been employed by the Auckland Exhibition Company which in turn had a contract with the Defence Department for the Blériot to make flights over the showgrounds.

There was also some friction between the Defence Department and the Exhibitions Company, although exactly why is unknown, but as a result the exhibition company cancelled its contract with Hammond as well, at which point control of the Blériot reverted to the Defence Department.

Shortly after the 28 January flight and the cancellation of the demonstration flight schedule, orders were given that the Blériot was to be dismantled and packed in its case and returned to Wellington. There it was put into storage while the government pondered what to do with it.

The solution to that became clear on 4 August 1914 when Britain declared war on Germany, which New Zealand followed the next day with its own declaration of war. The New Zealand Government immediately offered the Blériot to the British Government, which was accepted, and the aircraft left New Zealand in October 1914.

Hammond apparently stayed on in New Zealand until July when he returned to England and became an instructor with the Royal Flying Corps and was later posted to France. In 1916 he become involved in testing and evaluating new aircraft types, during which time he survived a number of aeroplane crashes.

In May 1918 he was in the United States with the British Aviation Mission and later with the US Liberty Loan War Bond drive, and again survived several crashes. But on 22 September 1918, his luck ran out, and he was killed when his Bristol Fighter F2B biplane crashed as it approached an airfield in Marion County, Indianapolis. He was 31. There were two passengers aboard the aeroplane with him, a local businessman who was also killed and a US Army Air lieutenant who was badly injured but survived.

Hammond's funeral in Indianapolis attracted thousands of people and included a guard of honour made up of British and American aviators. His body was cremated and his ashes were temporarily placed in the mausoleum belonging to the founder of the Indianapolis Speedway, Carl Fisher, awaiting collection by the family.

But it seems that never happened, and as far as it is known, the ashes remain in the mausoleum at Crown Hill Cemetery.

Following his death, his wife Ethelwyn returned to Seaford where she lived with her parents. She never remarried.

Perhaps the fact that his ashes were never collected indicates their marriage was not a success, perhaps exemplified by his exploits with Esmee McLennan.

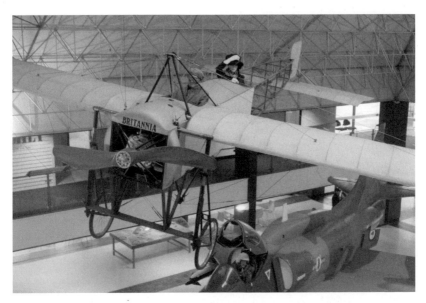

*A replica of the Blériot, complete with models of Joe Hammond and Esme McLennan hangs in the Royal New Zealand Air Force Museum at Wigram in Christchurch. The replica was built by David Comrie at his home in Dunedin.*
Air Force Museum of New Zealand, Wigram, Christchurch

# 1937

# SUICIDE BY AIR

Wairau Hospital theatre nurse Viva Farmar was setting off to the North Island for her annual two weeks' holiday on 8 February 1937 when she boarded a Marlborough Aero Club Waco aircraft at Ōmaka Aerodrome on the southwest outskirts of Blenheim.

But she never made her initial destination, Rongotai Airport in Wellington: her holiday journey ended when moments after take-off the 51-year-old threw herself out of the Waco after it flew over the coast and out into Cook Strait and plunged 750 metres to her death.

Viva Maud Farmar was a local and lived with her parents in Blenheim. She joined the staff at Blenheim's Wairau Hospital in 1906 as a student nurse, and after passing her nursing exams, she resigned in February 1910 and moved to Napier where she joined the staff of the Napier Hospital Board before switching to private nursing in 1911, which she did in New Zealand and later in England. She returned to New Zealand and Wairau Hospital as Sister in October 1914 after the First World War broke out, and during the war she was given leave of absence by the Board to undertake unspecified nursing war service in other parts of New Zealand, returning to Blenheim and Wairau Hospital in 1919. She was still employed at the hospital at the time of her death.

The Marlborough Aero Club was formed by a group of local aviation enthusiasts in 1928 who established their own aerodrome on land made available to them free of charge by the Omaka Domain Board that same year. The club's first aircraft was a Gypsy Moth loaned to them by the New Zealand Government.

Viva Farmar was one of the club's first and most enthusiastic members, joining in May 1929. She gained her 'A' pilot's licence in 1931, and soon after her licence was endorsed, enabling her to carry passengers. She was a keen aviator and made many flights across country and across Cook Strait on her own and with passengers. Reports from the era describe her as a skilful pilot with a natural aptitude and excellent judgement in handling aircraft. She was so good that she represented the club in several pageant competitions and was due to take part in a pageant at Whanganui two weeks after her death.

She was booked to fly from Blenheim to Wellington aboard a Cook Strait Airways flight on the morning of 8 February to begin her holiday, but early that morning she telephoned the Aero Club intending to charter one of the club's aircraft for the flight to Rongotai. When she was told that one of the club's pilots — Pilot Officer A.E. Willis — was flying over to Wellington in the club's Waco to pick up passengers and bring them back to Blenheim, she opted to join him on the flight over and cancelled her Cook Strait Airways booking.

Pilot Officer Willis picked Farmar up from her home and drove her out to the aerodrome, and he told investigators that on the way there she cheerfully discussed a tennis tournament that had been held the previous weekend

*Pilot Officer A.E. (Bill) Willis was at the controls of the Waco when Farmar leapt to her death. He later became Wing Commander and Commanding Officer, RNZAF Hobsonville. This photograph was taken in England about 1942 while his 489 Squadron was operating under the RAF Coastal Command.*

Air Force Museum of New Zealand, Wigram, Christchurch

between members of the Wellington and Marlborough Aero Clubs at the Blenheim tennis courts for which she had taken a leading part in arranging entertainment for the participants, including afternoon tea and supper.

'She talked of the weekend in a cheerful and vivacious way, displaying not the slightest sign that she was under any mental stress,' he said.

The pair took off from Ōmaka at 9.05 a.m. in the Waco, with Pilot Officer Willis at the controls and Farmar strapped into the seat beside him. At that point, Willis said that Farmar 'appeared to be her carefree self, joking in the most natural manner'. He later told investigators:

*We took off well and although there were a few bumps, we were getting along nicely until we were well over the strait. I think we were getting near to halfway over when she remarked that she wanted to get something from her handbag, which was lying on the rear seat. The movement necessary for her to get to her bag was very little, and I had not the slightest hesitation in allowing her to move, particularly as she had plenty of experience of travelling in the air.*

*She shifted to the rear seat, and the next I knew was that there was a draught in the aeroplane. I looked around and found that the door was open, and Miss Farmar was in the act of jumping. I tried to reach her but she eluded me and she went through the door before I could do anything more. The whole thing happened almost in a second. I got the aeroplane into control again. It needed immediate attention, and I followed her all the way to the sea by circling. We were at about 2500 feet and I went down, I should say, to about 50 feet above the water but she had hit the sea sometime before I could get down, but I could see perfectly and she just went in and disappeared. The sea was pretty rough with white horses everywhere.*

*I flew around for some time but couldn't see a sign of her and then decided that the only thing I could do was to get back to Blenheim as soon as I could and report the whole thing.*

Civil aviation authorities grounded the Waco until it could be inspected, which occurred the next day when Willis took off again with a Government aviation inspector, a local police constable and the president of the Aero Club aboard to check the door in flight. No fault was found with the door, and officials were surprised that she was actually able to open it in flight in the face of resistance from the outside slipstream.

Viva Farmar's body was never recovered from Cook Strait, and the reasons behind her unique suicide — the only one recorded in New Zealand aviation history — have never been established. Family and friends were unable to proffer any cause for her actions, but her death deeply affected Pilot Officer Willis, as well as her work colleagues and family.

*This is the Marlborough Aero Club Waco aircraft from which Viva Farmar leapt to her death in Cook Strait in 1937. The photograph was probably taken in 1936 at Rongotai, now Wellington International Airport.*
Walsh Memorial Library, The Museum of Transport & Technology (MOTAT)

The Waco was built by the Waco Aircraft Company in Ohio, USA and was imported for the Marlborough Aero Club in 1936. At the outbreak of the Second World War in 1939 it was impressed into service with the Royal New Zealand Air Force as NZ575 and allocated to the Communications Flight, based at Rongotai. After the war it was declared surplus and returned to the Marlborough Aero Club as ZK-ALA. In 1947 it was damaged in a crash landing and was sold to Blackmore Air Services in Rotorua which repaired the aircraft and used it for charter and tourism flights. In 1951 that company was taken over by James Aviation Ltd, and after another crash landing in 1958 the aircraft was written off and sold to G.E. Giltrap Ltd in Rotorua and displayed in a vintage car collection at Rotorua Airport. The following year it was sent to Coolangatta in Queensland with the rest of the collection. It then passed through several owners until it was partially restored to flying condition by South Pacific Airmotive at Camden, New South Wales. Thereafter it languished, hidden away, until in 2008 it was purchased by Jay McIntyre, Stuart Leslie and Rex Newman and returned to Blenheim where it underwent a full restoration by the three partners at Omaka Airport. In January 2023, a restored ZK-AEL took to the air again, as shown below, photographed during a test flight.

Classic Air Photography, Blenheim

# Religion

# 1868

# RELIGIOUS BIGOTRY ALIVE AND WELL IN COLONIAL NEW ZEALAND

Many early European settlers came to New Zealand to leave behind unhealthy overcrowding, class distinctions and lack of opportunities. Often, however, they brought with them the religious intolerance, bigotry and political divisions that marred their homelands.

And in no area was this more obvious than in the intolerance between Irish and British Protestants, and Irish Roman Catholics, which resulted in widespread disputes and fighting in many parts of New Zealand, particularly in the goldfield areas where there were large numbers of Irish Catholics.

Thousands of Irish came to New Zealand after 1850 attracted by the goldfields in Otago and on the West Coast.

Many felt they were exiles from their homeland, driven out by ongoing famine and repressive and unscrupulous absentee English landlords. They brought with them many of the customs and traditions of their homeland including their Roman Catholic religious beliefs and celebrations like St Patrick's Day.

Many also brought strongly held views on Irish republicanism and a strong hatred of the English, and very often they were not slow to express those views which created tension in the communities in which they lived.

But they were a minority within their communities, making up about a third of the population, the rest being mainly English and Scots.

The causes of the quarrels were usually religion and the Irish campaign for home rule of Northern Ireland.

Violence first broke out on the shores of Lake Wakatipu in Central Otago in about 1863, when thousands of goldminers from Australia and California descended on the area after gold was found in the Arrow River in 1862.

Early Wakatipu settler and author Alfred Duncan recounted how a drunken brawl broke out between Catholic Irish goldminers and other diggers, with some ghastly wounds inflicted by savagely swung shovels and other makeshift weapons.

In 1865, at the South Westland goldfield of Ōkārito, fighting broke out between Irish Catholics and Protestants, eventually leading to a hotel and store being damaged and several people being badly wounded with claw-hammers, sluice forks and stones.

Further violence followed in March 1867 at Ahaura on the banks of the Grey River where there was long-standing tension between Irish Catholic and English prospectors. That came to an end when the Irish ringleaders were arrested and taken to Greymouth prison.

Public protest and fundraising meetings and marches were regularly held by Irish Catholics at the mining settlements of Charleston and Hokitika. The level of Irish support for the republican cause is probably evidenced by the fact that the Irish miners at Ōkārito gave a total of £243 — a considerable sum at that time — as a donation to Irish republican supporters being held prisoner in England.

There were also reports of fighting between Protestant and Catholic Irish miners at Thames in the spring of 1869.

An already tense situation on the West Coast was worsened by two events overseas which set the scene for a final showdown.

In 1867, republican supporters in Ireland, known as Fenians, staged uprisings against the English who at the time governed the whole of Ireland, unrest that was harshly suppressed. (The term Fenian originated from the mythical hunter-warrior of Ireland, Fionn mac Cumhaill, more commonly known in other parts of the world as Finn McCool.)

The Fenian ringleaders were arrested and taken to Manchester where their supporters tried to free them by attacking a prison van, killing a police sergeant in the process. Three of the attackers were convicted of murder and hanged at Salford in November 1867. They became known as the Manchester Martyrs.

In the following month Fenians exploded a bomb at Clerkenwell Prison in London, in an attempt to free one of their members. The attempt failed but killed twelve innocent Londoners and injured 120 others in their homes nearby, which enraged the English public and hardened attitudes towards the Irish.

Back in New Zealand on 3 March 1868, a crowd of about 800 Irish Catholics, headed by the controversial republican priest, Irishman Father William Larkin, paraded through the streets of Hokitika and broke into the town's cemetery where they erected a wooden Celtic cross in honour of the Manchester Martyrs. At the cemetery the priest and a Catholic Irish journalist — John Manning — addressed the crowd, speaking out against the New Zealand Government. Larkin and Manning were behind the strongly Irish nationalist weekly newspaper, *The New Zealand Celt*, which first appeared on the West Coast in August 1867.

During the protest, Larkin reportedly recited the Catholic burial service in Latin and led the crowd in prayer, then reminded them of Ireland's grievances and commended the courage shown by 'the three martyrs' before erecting the memorial cross.

Larkin was reputedly related to one of the Manchester Martyrs and was a determined supporter of Irish nationalism, which ultimately saw him run afoul of the Roman Catholic Church in New Zealand for a period and led to his suspension from priestly duties. Manning had been a journalist with *The Ballarat Times* in Australia and had been involved in the Battle of the Eureka Stockade (December 1854) which resulted in him facing trial for treason in Melbourne in February 1855.

A few days after the Hokitika cemetery parade, on St Patrick's Day — 17 March — another demonstration by Irish Catholics took place in Westport.

Five days earlier, on 12 March 1868, Irishman Henry O'Farrell had attempted to assassinate the Duke of Edinburgh, Prince Alfred, while he was on a visit to Australia. He was shot in the back while attending a fair at Clontarf in Sydney but survived. Politicians in Australia and New Zealand were quick to capitalise on the attack to advance campaigns against the Irish and against Catholics.

When news of the assassination attempt reached New Zealand, things quickly came to a head on the West Coast. Leaders of the Irish Catholic community were arrested on charges of seditious libel and rioting and were imprisoned or fined.

On 3 April, a group of about 170 English and Scottish miners returned to their homes at Addison's Flat about 13 kilometres south of Westport, after attending festivities in Westport to celebrate the Duke of Edinburgh's survival from the assassination attempt.

The marchers carried a large British standard with a crown of flowers and foliage, and with an orange base. They were reportedly led by a woman riding a white horse, a reference to the fact that in the 1690 Battle of the Boyne, the Protestant King William III — William of Orange — rode a white horse into battle against the forces of the deposed Catholic King James II. William was victorious, a victory that was critical in ensuring the continued ascendancy of Protestantism in Ireland.

The banner, the patriotic singing and the white horse were too much of a provocation for the town's Irish Catholics, later described as Fenian sympathisers, who attacked the marchers with stones and fists and quickly broke up the parade.

The loyalists fled back to Westport where they told authorities of the attack, claiming that a riot had occurred.

The authorities were quick to act, fearing a Fenian uprising was under way. Eight hundred special constables were sworn in at Hokitika and Westport, and 40 members of the Armed Constabulary from Hokitika were summoned, while the Governor, Sir George Bowen, dispatched a company of the 18th Royal Irish Regiment from Wellington by sea.

Meanwhile at Addison's Flat, rumours were spreading that the special constables were coming to retaliate, and a large force of Irish Catholic defenders from all around the area had gathered to meet them, armed with whatever weapons they could find.

The facts and precise details about the Addison's Flat riot have largely been lost in the rhetoric expressed by both sides, but one thing that is clear is the impact of the actions of one man, the Nelson Southwest Goldfields chief warden, Thomas Kynnersley.

Born in Staffordshire, England, Kynnersley had joined the Royal Navy as a youngster and was commissioned lieutenant at the age of 21. He served on various ships including HMS *Orpheus* which had been assigned to the Australia Station. He was dogged with ill-health and granted leave from the Navy, settling at Pelorus Sound where, in 1864, he was appointed Warden of the Pelorus Goldfield. When that claim ran out, he was transferred to the West Coast as Warden of the Nelson goldfield and Resident Magistrate at Cobden. He later established his headquarters at Charleston and then Westport, and in 1867 was appointed Chief Warden and Commissioner of the Nelson Southwest Goldfields, with full control over the goldfields and the power to spend public money on public works.

Some accounts of the Addison's Flat event say that when the special forces arrived a battle ensued in which the loyalist forces were driven back into a swamp about two miles from town, at which point Thomas Kynnersley arrived on horseback, rode into the fray and calmed the situation, bringing hostilities to an end.

Other accounts make no mention of that alleged confrontation but say Kynnersley rode to Addison's Flat accompanied by a few policemen after the loyalists had arrived back at Westport, and that he sent a dispatch rider back to Westport to report that all was quiet and peaceful at Addison's Flat, and that no further forces were needed, and no government action was to be initiated.

Next day there was agitation among the miners at Westport to march to Addison's Flat to avenge the 'indignation against the men who had insulted loyalty and to redress the wrongs' they felt had been inflicted, but they were talked out of further action by Kynnersley who had returned to Westport.

On the evening of Saturday, 11 April, Kynnersley was once again in Addison's Flat where he attended a meeting of the local citizenry at the Daniel O'Connell Hotel. In the meeting unanimous resolutions of loyalty to the Crown and 'an honourable peace' were passed by popular vote.

At the time Kynnersley was 29 and his actions made him famous. He is remembered for 'quelling, single-handed, the Fenian riot which flared at Addison's Flat' while other accounts depict him as restoring

*Members of three lodges of the Loyal Orange Order along with members of the Ancient Order of Foresters gather at Charleston on Monday, 13 April 1868, in what was a demonstration of loyalty to Queen Victoria following the assassination attempt on the Duke of Edinburgh, Prince Alfred, in Sydney by Irish radical Henry O'Farrell. A crowd estimated at more than 1000 people from a large number of local organisations took part in a parade, sporting flags and banners, and led by a military band. They marched from the Hokitika Municipal Reserve where a ceremonial tree planting took place, through the streets of the town and finally to the Duke of Edinburgh Theatre where a large free lunch banquet took place with some 1200 people taking part in shifts. The banner on the left refers to three Lodges of the Orange Order: the Loyal Charleston Lodge No. 5583, the Loyal Westport Lodge No. 5562 and the Loyal Reefton Lodge No. 5931. The second banner on the right is the Court Royal Oak No. 6532 of the Ancient Order of Foresters. Its presence at the occasion is a mystery, as this Court (Lodge) is recorded as being based in Wyndham in Southland. The* Grey River Argus *reported that numbers joining the demonstration 'greatly exceeded that of the recent processions of Fenian sympathisers' and that 'the greatest enthusiasm prevailed'. The gathering happened just a few days after the Battle of Addison's Flat.*

Denniston Miners Collection. Ref: 1/2-048992-F, Alexander Turnbull Library, Wellington, New Zealand

order while standing on a rock amid a swamp while the two sides fought it out.

The issue was not helped by the newspapers of the time.

Kynnersley himself was critical of *The Westport Times,* which he accused of stoking the trouble by its reporting of anti-Irish speeches made at a loyalty rally in Westport on 2 April. The Catholic weekly the *New Zealand Celt* also came in for its share of criticism over its strident support for Irish republicanism and the Manchester Martyrs.

While the Addison's Flat incident was settled, the animosity between Irish Catholics and English loyalists on the Coast continued to simmer for years, involving numerous court cases, the West Coast newspapers of the day and even stretched as far as local body politics.

Nor was it the end of anti-Catholic sentiment in New Zealand.

On Boxing Day 1879 there was rioting in the streets of Christchurch when a group of Catholic Irish railway workers armed with pickaxe handles attacked a parade of Orangemen marching down Manchester Street in the city. The procession involved men from the local Orange Lodge, an international Protestant fraternal organisation opposed to Irish republicanism, and which claimed to defend Protestant civil and religious freedoms.

Police struggled to control the riot because they were short-handed after 21 of their number had been dispatched to Timaru where another confrontation was looming. However, aided by a Roman Catholic priest, they did manage to separate the warring factions, but not before some of the Orangemen had been badly hurt. Police arrested four of the Irishmen on the day and later another fourteen were arrested. Four were sentenced to eighteen months' jail with hard labour, and twelve were given sentences of twelve months with hard labour.

Meanwhile in Timaru a confrontation was under way between local Irishmen and Protestant Orangemen from the Timaru Orange Lodge.

The Irish very strongly opposed a proposed processional march by Lodge members through the streets of Timaru and besieged the Orangemen in the Forresters Hall in the town, despite efforts of local police and nineteen reinforcements called in from Christchurch to keep the peace.

A local magistrate was called in to read the Riot Act, a British law which allowed local authorities to declare a public gathering unlawful and ordering the assembly to disperse or face punitive action. But the Irishmen refused to leave until they were given an assurance that the procession would not go ahead, an assurance that was duly given. Six of the Irishmen were arrested during the confrontation but were later released under good behaviour bonds.

The peace in both towns was uneasy, and in Timaru further police were called in from Dunedin and Ōamaru, and a 51-strong detachment from the Armed Constabulary in Wellington was sent to ensure there was no further trouble.

Nothing remains of Addison's Flat today, apart from the cemetery. But at the time of the so-called Battle of Addison's Flat, the town had a population of about 5000 people. It was named after Arthur Addison, known at the time as Darkie Addison, a former African American slave who prospected and found gold in the area near Charleston in 1867.

# 1875

# HEROIC MARTYRDOM IN KAIAPOI

Parishioners of the Anglican parish of Kaiapoi, north of Christchurch, kicked off a controversy on 15 November 1875 that was to rebound about the Anglican Church of New Zealand for months, finally ending in their curate being convicted of a raft of doctrinal charges and suspended.

The parishioners complained to the Bishop of Christchurch, Henry Harper, that their new parish priest, the Rev. H.E. Carlyon, was 'adoring the sacrament' and urging the confession of sins, acts which were too close to Catholicism for their comfort.

Their complaint was the first and only ritualistic controversy in the Anglican Church in New Zealand.

The Rev. Hubert Edward Carlyon was a young English priest, a recently ordained graduate of Cambridge University who had served the Church in Cornwall.

He arrived in Lyttelton aboard the sailing ship *Cicero* along with 221 other emigrants, on 18 May 1875. His first act for the Church was to join a festival at the Holy Trinity Church at Lyttelton on Sunday, 23 May to celebrate the dedication of the church, and after that he joined his new parish at Kaiapoi.

While he was seen by the Church hierarchy in New Zealand as a diligent and hard-working priest, he was known to belong to the High Church side of the Church of England and had adopted many of the practices of the ritualists in his Cornwall parish and was keen to introduce these to his new parishioners at Kaiapoi. They were apparently unaware of his intentions.

Carlyon was introduced to his parishioners on 4 June 1875 and made plain to them that he intended to make some changes to the services, changes which he said had been approved by Bishop Harper.

One of the changes he proposed making was to the ceremony of Communion, and this and his other proposed changes were narrowly approved by the Kaiapoi vestry.

Ritualism in the Church of England was an issue at the time. It related to the way churches carried out their public worship and the rituals and ceremonies they used. Its proponents wanted more use of both ritual and ceremony in their churches and the reintroduction of some of the Roman Catholic liturgical practices, while those opposed saw it as an unwelcome and unwanted return to the practices of the Roman Catholic Church that had been dropped during the reign of Henry VIII.

*Kaiapoi as it was about 1900, with two unidentified churches on the left — perhaps one of them was at the centre of the Carlyon martyrdom?*

Kaiapoi by Burton Brothers. Ref: C.014081, Te Papa Tongarewa Museum of New Zealand

It was often also associated with the differences between what was known as the High Church (which emphasised formality and adherence to custom) and the Low Church (which placed little emphasis on rituals and sacraments).

It was an issue that raged in the Anglican Church in New Zealand for many years.

Nothing happened for the first few weeks after Carlyon's arrival at Kaiapoi, but when he did finally introduce changes to the ceremonies of worship in early July, opposition began to mount to his ideas, leading to one vestryman resigning in protest.

A special general meeting of the parishioners was called to elect a replacement vestryman, but the gathering decided against replacing him until after a debate could be held on what was happening within the parish and an inquiry held into the conduct of the new parish priest.

When the details of the dispute reached Bishop Harper, he set up a Commission of Inquiry headed by the Dean of Christchurch, Henry Jacobs. He was the second most senior clergyman after the bishop himself.

Jacobs called a meeting of the parish on 22 November to outline how the inquiry would work and endeavour to keep everyone calm. But his attempts failed and the meeting because acrimonious and disorderly, with bitter personal attacks being flung about.

Some felt the meeting itself had the right to judge Carlyon's conduct without interference from the bishop, while others felt the issues should go before a properly constituted Court of Inquiry.

Finally, there was agreement that the proposed inquiry should go ahead, and it did that very night and continued four days later.

There was a mass of charges to be decided, some relating to what were considered errors in doctrine, others to ceremonial matters within the parish. Yet others related to more obscure Church matters such as confessions, baptisms, the role of the Virgin Mary, and esoteric beliefs such as whether the dead could pray for the living.

Carlyon faced a string of accusations including that he had been whispering secret prayers during the creed, crossing himself, and 'engaging in idolatrous adoration of the consecrated elements'.

The fiercest controversy, however, revolved around charges relating to self-examination and confession — apparently all to do with privately dealing with one's own 'sins' in direct and personal communication with God, or confessing one's sins openly to a priest.

Carlyon himself was subject to intense examination and cross-examination during the inquiry, and later studies concluded that, by and large, the evidence supported him.

The Commission of Inquiry handed its conclusions to the bishop for him to consider, and it was at that point that things began to fall apart.

It started when two newspapers, *The Press* and *The Lyttelton Times*, because of some misunderstanding, published material from the inquiry before it could be handed over to the bishop.

The biggest controversy concerned evidence given about Carlyon's practice of mixing water with the Communion wine, which he said had been sanctioned by the bishop. The problem was that Harper had earlier indicated to a Church synod meeting that it was not acceptable.

Carlyon's evidence was that he had twice raised the matter with Harper in writing, asking him to sanction the practice: in response to the first letter the bishop had declined to sanction it but said he wasn't against the idea. In response to the second letter, he declared that he would not object to Carlyon continuing to add water, as long as the vestry had agreed to it.

*Bishop Henry Harper, Warden of Christ's College, the first Anglican Bishop of Christchurch, and from 1868 until 1890 primate of the Anglican Church in New Zealand, who became deeply embroiled in the Carlyon ritualistic controversy that engulfed the church in Canterbury, and who eventually formally dismissed the recalcitrant curate in 1877.*

Photographed in 1868 by Dr Alfred Charles Barker. Wikimedia Commons

Harper met with the Kaiapoi vestry on 20 December, and later wrote that he felt Carlyon had acted injudiciously in some cases, but he should remain curate of Kaiapoi.

That didn't please many of the parishioners, and at the midnight service on 31 January 1875, Carlyon's sermon was suddenly interrupted by loud drumming and bell ringing outside the church. That created chaos within, with some women parishioners fainting. Some of the men in the congregation rushed outside where they found two men with drums and bells and saw others fleeing the scene. A fracas ensued between the protestors and the churchmen, and the drum was damaged.

The bishop appealed for tolerance over the dispute, saying Carlyon would remain at his post, but at the same time charging him with 'errors in doctrine concerning the conditions of departing souls, the ceremonial and sacramental character of Christ's religion and ministry, and the nature of the ministry of reconciliation'.

On 14 January, Bishop Harper formally wrote to Carlyon asking him to desist from a number of his actions such as mixing water with the wine, and to stop his practice of 'elevating the chalice during the prayer of consecration' as part of the Communion sacrament.

That didn't satisfy the objectors, and on 24 January the vestry reconvened their adjourned special meeting to discuss the bishop's response, many feeling that the decision on Carlyon's future was theirs to make and not the bishop's. Eventually they passed a motion calling for Carlyon to resign, and insisting that if he didn't, the matter be laid before the Standing Committee of the Synod, the governing body of the Anglican Church in New Zealand.

The meeting ended acrimoniously and with bitter feelings all round.

On 31 January, the vestry met again and drew Carlyon's attention to its 24 January resolution calling for him to resign. Another vestryman presented a petition to Carlyon, signed by some 70 parishioners, asking him not to resign. Carlyon told the meeting that he had no intention of resigning.

Meanwhile, the controversy had grown into a much wider argument with two local Anglican journals, the *Church Magazine* and the *Church News*, the official organ of the Kaiapoi diocese, entering the fray, criticising the bishop for his handling of the issue and calling for Carlyon's resignation. Both magazines published lengthy articles attacking Carlyon's doctrines, with the *Church News* declaring 'there will be no peace for the parish of Kaiapoi, or the diocese of Christchurch, so long as he holds this present office.'

That meant that *Church News*, the official bulletin of the Kaiapoi diocese, was in direct and open conflict with the official view of the diocese itself.

Things went from bad to worse when the bishop's son, who was the Archdeacon of Timaru, wrote a letter to *The Lyttelton Times* and *The Press* openly questioning his father's rulings.

And so it dragged on for weeks with the issues and arguments for and against openly debated in the newspapers, and with disputes over loyalties and who was siding with whom argued at countless committee meetings and debates.

Finally, the anti-Carlyonists — irked by his refusal to resign — sent a deputation to the Synod's Standing Committee armed with a petition signed by more than 100 supporters, calling on the Synod to ask Carlyon to resign. The committee refused on the grounds that they had not been asked by the bishop to assist him resolving the issue.

Harper told the deputation in effect that if their complaint against Carlyon was on the grounds of doctrine, under Church rules they should seek an Ecclesiastical Court hearing, and that was what happened.

The anti-Carlyonists were boycotting his Sunday services, and some signed a petition asking a church warden and lay preacher to take alternative services in the nearby Orange Lodge Hall. Others wanted the bishop to take the Easter service at Kaiapoi and administer Communion to them because they wouldn't take it from Carlyon.

But Carlyon wasn't without some support among the congregation and at the 1875 annual general meeting, several of his supporters were elected to warden positions and to the vestry, at which point the anti-Carlyonists walked out of the meeting.

The church's news bulletin, The *Church News*, went on the attack again, accusing Carlyon and his supporters of stacking the meeting with ring-ins. They claimed 'the majority was made up, to a considerable extent, of persons registered for the occasion, who not only were unknown as resident churchmen but in some cases were only too well known as persons of disreputable character'.

The battle raged on between supporters and the church news bulletin, and between Carlyon and the bishop, with both sides becoming more entrenched and their differences increasing despite attempts by many to calm things down.

Finally, in September 1876, accusations against Carlyon were formally laid by his opponents.

He was charged before the Church's Chancellor with twelve offences relating to some of the mystical beliefs of Christians concerning the sacrament, with teaching the need for confessions to a priest, and of 'adoring the sacrament after consecration'.

The chancellor was apparently unsure of what steps he should take and sought legal advice, which was that he should place the charges before the diocesan Court of Assessors, which he did in December. The task of the Assessors' Court was to determine if the charges could be proved, and if they could, to put the case before the Bench of Bishops to decide.

The court decided that eleven of the charges could be proven — or had been admitted by Carlyon — and the case was put before the Bench of Bishops, which consisted of the Bishops of Auckland, Wellington, Christchurch and Dunedin.

The level of pettiness was typified by the fact that Carlyon was charged before the Kaiapoi Magistrates Court with allowing a horse to obstruct a footpath — he was charged and convicted by the magistrate who was one of his foremost opponents in the parish.

On Easter Monday, 1877, the annual meeting of the parish was held, and this time the anti-Carlyonists triumphed, with seven of their supporters elected to the vestry, and only one Carlyon supporter.

Thereafter affairs in the parish continued to plummet with continual arguments over issues of doctrine and ritual, and with the financial position of the parish deteriorating. At one stage matters of ritual reached such a low point that some opponents threatened physical violence before the altar during a service to make their point.

On 17 September 1877, the Bench of Bishops announced their decision — they had found Carlyon guilty of maintaining unauthorised doctrines and practices and summoned him to appear before them on 10 October to hear his sentence.

He had been found guilty of seven of the twelve charges.

At his sentencing at the library of Christ's College school in Christchurch, about 50 people gathered to witness the event.

The findings of the Bench of Bishops were read to him, and Carlyon responded with a lengthy defence.

On three of the charges to do with administering the sacrament, he was admonished by the bishops and ordered to desist in his practices, and on two other charges he was suspended for one month from the ministry of the church, the suspension to continue until he formally retracted his errors.

The decision didn't go down well with Carlyon's supporters at Kaiapoi. A large protest meeting was held at the Kaiapoi Institute on 19 October and a petition was organised protesting at the Bench of Bishop's decision, calling it unjust, impolitic and doctrinally unsound. The signatories declared that if the decision was upheld, they would resign from the Church.

Meanwhile negotiations continued between Bishop Harper and Carlyon to try to reach agreement on how Carlyon could retract his 'erroneous doctrine'. They weren't able to do so, however, and on 15 November, Harper wrote to Carlyon telling him to resign his position or face dismissal.

Carlyon ignored that letter and instead sought two years' leave of absence.

Bishop Harper then called a meeting of the Synod's Standing Committee and sought their views on dismissing Carlyon. The meeting agreed he should go, and on 23 November 1877, Bishop Harper formally dismissed Carlyon.

But by then Carlyon had already returned to England. He told his Kaiapoi supporters that he would not resign, that he was going to

England to seek the advice of Church of England theologians there and would return.

Harper meanwhile appointed a replacement.

Carlyon's mission to England ended in defeat when he was not supported by the theologians he consulted. Consequently, on 20 July 1878, he wrote to Harper retracting his errors.

Later that year Carlyon moved to South Africa where he spent the next ten years in various church posts, and where he married an English-born widow, Marie Tatham. The couple returned to England in 1889 where he spent the rest of his life until his death in 1900. His widow died in Bromley, Kent, in 1922.

# 1917

# WARTIME CENSOR AND POST OFFICE ACCUSED OF CATHOLIC BIAS

The Reform/Liberal Government set up a Royal Commission of Inquiry on 25 July 1917, to investigate allegations that the Post Office censor was using his position to suppress anti-Roman Catholic activities.

The allegations had been made by the Rev. Howard Elliot, a former pastor of the Mt Eden Baptist Church in Auckland and founder of the right-wing Protestant Political Association, who alleged that Roman Catholic forces within the Auckland Post Office were interfering with his mail.

Elliot was born in Maldon, Victoria, in 1877 and was brought up as a Methodist but trained for the Baptist ministry and held a number of pastorates in Australia. He was serving as secretary of the Queensland Baptist Union from 1906 to 1909 when he was invited to take up the pastorship of the large Mt Eden Baptist Church.

He had earned a reputation in Australia for creating sectarian controversy and it wasn't long before he was doing the same in Auckland.

He was a founder member of the National Schools Defence League which opposed plans by the Bible in State Schools League of New Zealand for the introduction of religious education into primary schools. They were concerned that the major denominations would dictate the instruction, and that it might lead to the government granting state funds to schools run by the Roman Catholic Church and to other private schools.

During his time as pastor of the Mt Eden Baptist Church, his sermons regularly asserted that there was a Catholic and Irish conspiracy to take over the New Zealand civil service, particularly education and the police.

In 1912, he became secretary of the Auckland Auxiliary of the Baptist Union of New Zealand, a post he resigned in 1917 when he founded the Protestant Political Association. This organisation was closely aligned with the Loyal Orange Institute of New Zealand, a strident anti-Catholic organisation that originated in Northern Ireland in 1795 and was dedicated to defending Protestant civil and religious liberties.

*Howard Elliot – 'deserved all he got and a good deal more'.*

Public domain, via Wikimedia Commons

The Order began in New Zealand in 1858 and at one stage had 47 'lodges' throughout the country.

Elliot became a full-time organiser for the Protestant Political Association, touring the country addressing crowds on his sectarian views and publishing supporting pamphlets. His themes included claims that Roman Catholics were dominating the New Zealand civil service, that the Pope and the Vatican were responsible for the First World War and that the Roman Catholic Church was disloyal because it supported home rule for Ireland and was opposed to its seminarians and brothers being conscripted for war service. He was also strongly opposed to socialism and organised labour, and to the Labour Party which was formally founded on 7 July 1916.

To an extent parts of the Roman Catholic Church, particularly the Catholic weekly newspaper *The Tablet* and the Catholic Federation, added fuel to Elliot's rise to influence.

*The Tablet* was edited by Dr James Kelly, an Irish-born former Ōpunake parish priest and an outspoken and passionate Irish nationalist with strong anti-British opinions and a strident commitment to Irish nationalism. He once famously described Queen Victoria as a 'fat old German woman'.

Kelly used the newspaper to promote his strongly held opinions and was uncompromising in his condemnation of those he saw as enemies of Ireland and his Roman Catholic faith. He was a strong supporter of the Sinn Fein movement, which was involved in Ireland's 1916 Easter Uprising, and he used his editorial powers in *The Tablet* to encourage Irish Catholics to join the movement.

The New Zealand Catholic Federation was formed in 1912–13 following the foundation of similar organisations in Europe and Australia. It lobbied for Catholic interests, notably to push for government support for Catholic schools and to oppose the Protestant-inspired Bible in Schools campaign.

At the time Roman Catholics made up less than 13 per cent of New Zealand's non-Māori population, and the outward display of Catholic assertiveness,

*Dr James Kelly, the Irish-born former priest and editor of* The Tablet. *Kelly was an outspoken and passionate Irish nationalist with strong anti-British opinions. He used the newspaper to promote his opinions and to condemn those he saw as enemies of Ireland and his Roman Catholic faith.*

Puke Ariki Feaver collection

as reflected in the columns in *The Tablet* and the actions of the Catholic Federation, caused concern to the Protestant and non-conformist majority. It also helped to inspire the Orange Lodge and Elliot to form the Protestant Political Association to oppose them.

In a speech to hundreds of Association supporters at the Auckland Town Hall on 11 July 1917, Elliot detailed a long list of quite absurd allegations against the Catholic Church and against the Post Office. These included claims that:

- Catholics could get anything in the daily press, but Protestants could get practically nothing.
- A Catholic priest in Greymouth had been charged with stealing £750, but the jury was warned off by 'a certain organisation' and subsequently returned a not-guilty verdict.
- A nun in Taumarunui had drowned herself after becoming pregnant.
- The body of a dead baby was found on the grounds of an Auckland convent.
- Some convents had lime pits to dispose of the bodies of unwanted babies.

There were also insinuations about drunken priests.

Elliot claimed that there was corruption in the Post Office, alleging that military censors were interfering with the delivery of his mail on the instructions of the Roman Catholic Church.

He told the supporters that the censors had tried to stifle the Town Hall meeting by opening envelopes containing invitations to the meeting and removing them, claiming that other letters had not been delivered in time for recipients to receive the invitations before the meeting took place.

Tickets and invitations to the meeting sent to Protestant clergymen in the city, in plenty of time for delivery, had been held up he claimed, which also meant that church congregations could not be advised of the planned meeting during Sunday church services.

Elliot's campaign to promote sectarian hatred against Catholics

## The Triple Alliance

WARDISM — ROMANISM — BOLSHEVISM

*This cartoon appeared in the* NZ Truth *newspaper in December 1919 during the election campaign. It suggests that both the Labour Party, represented by Bolshevism, and Joseph Ward's Liberal Party were controlled by the Roman Catholic Church.*

Papers Past, National Library of New Zealand

gathered thousands of supporters and he was producing thousands of pamphlets — one entitled 'Rome's Hideous Guilt in the European Carnage' — and a regular newsletter called *The Sentinel*. Some of these publications caught the attention of the wartime censor.

A Post Office mailbox used by Elliot, the Protestant Political Association and the Orange Lodge had attracted the attention of the censor because of the activities of both the Association and the Lodge. Elliot told the meeting that many letters concerning the subject of Roman Catholicism had not been delivered to the box but had been held up by the censor.

He also alleged that during the 1917 Auckland City Council elections letters from the Orange Lodge's Protestant Vigilance Committee had been interfered with by the censor 'entirely in the interest of the Roman Catholics'. The Reform Prime Minister was William Massey, an Ulster Protestant and a former member of the Orange Lodge. He was also an Oddfellow and a Freemason, and was strongly opposed to organised labour. On 11 July, the government announced that a full inquiry into the allegations would be made and subsequently appointed Christchurch magistrate Mr H.W. Bishop as the Commissioner.

*Reform Party prime minister, William Massey, an Ulster Protestant and Orangeman, who is said to have had a 'natural empathy' with Howard Elliot and was a strong opponent of organised labour.*

Harris & Ewing, public domain, via Wikimedia Commons

The inquiry opened in Auckland on 13 August 1917 with lawyers representing the government and Post Office, the Protestant Political Association and Elliot. After two weeks of evidence the Royal Commission's report was tabled in Parliament, with Bishop finding no evidence of impropriety or corruption on the part of the Auckland postal officials.

In reporting his findings the Commissioner said, after reviewing all the evidence exhaustively, 'The public may rest assured that the very high reputation that the Postal Department has always enjoyed in this Dominion, as one of the most important Departments of State, has not in any way been lessened by the result of this inquiry.'

He dismissed Elliot's accusations as an ill-advised, ill-bred and reckless attack on a public department, accusing him of 'concocting abominable and disgusting allegations'. He said Elliot was saturated with sectarian bitterness, had lost all sense of propriety and could not appreciate the invidious position he had placed himself with his allegations.

Newspaper editorials widely welcomed the findings but criticised the government for going ahead with the inquiry in the first place.

Predictably the findings met with outrage by Elliot and his supporters. The Wellington Ministers' Association half-heartedly passed a resolution in support of his beliefs and his bona fides, but they went no further.

A meeting of his Protestant Political Association protested that the findings were 'against the weight of the evidence', and that unwarrantable censorship operated in the interests of the Roman Catholic Church. The meeting passed a resolution protesting against the refusal of Cabinet to appoint a Supreme Court Judge to conduct an inquiry into the inquiry.

Elliot held extreme views but is said to have had a natural empathy with William Massey and appears to have had an inexplicable and unwarranted level of influence on the Reform Government.

The Protestant Political Association was actively involved in the 1919 and 1922 general elections, endorsing the Reform Party's candidates. In 1920, the Reform Government passed two pieces of legislation that would seem to have aligned with Elliot's philosophies, withdrawing government-paid scholarships to private schools and overruling a 1907 Vatican decree which insisted that, to be valid, marriages between Catholics and non-Catholics had to be witnessed by a Catholic priest.

In 1919 Elliot claimed the Protestant Political Association had a membership of 200,000 people, but as wartime restrictions and tensions eased after the end of the war, interest in him and the association began to wane. A turning point was probably a 1924 public meeting at the Empress Theatre in Wellington, organised by the leader of the Parliamentary Labour Party, Harry Holland, who Elliot strongly opposed.

*Harry Holland photographed in 1922, when he was leader of the Labour Party, and Member of Parliament for Buller.*

S.P. Andrew Ltd via Wikimedia Commons

In 1923, King George V had gone to Rome and had met with Pope Pius XI. Elliot accused the king of colluding with the Roman Catholic Church against the Empire, leading Holland to describe Elliot in Parliament as 'one of the most disloyal men in New Zealand'.

Elliot challenged Holland to repeat his accusation outside Parliament where he would not enjoy parliamentary privilege. Holland did so in July 1924 at the Empress Theatre, which was filled with thousands of people, with hundreds more turned away because it was full, and there he presented a long list of Elliot's writings and sayings, which he claimed proved his disloyalty and sedition beyond doubt.

Holland's actions spelled the death knell of Elliot's Protestant Political Association and by the end of 1929 it had run out of steam and supporters.

But it wasn't the end of Elliot. He continued his agitation against organised labour and the Catholic Church. In 1929 he was objecting to the school dental scheme being extended to include private schools. Without the base of the association's supporters, he turned to publishing to expound his views, establishing a monthly newspaper, *The New Zealand Financial Times*, in 1930. He also became the editor of *The Nation*, the magazine of the Orange Lodge organisation. Both publications provided him with outlets for his anti-Catholic and anti-labour views, but neither lasted.

Elliot finally retired to Te Awamutu where he died in November 1956.

Elliot's allegation about the death of the nun at Taumarunui aroused the ire of the dead woman's brother, 21-year-old Christopher Clements. He had served as a frontline soldier and had been gassed and wounded during the Battle of Messines in Belgium in June 1917. He returned home from the war in September and read reports of Elliot's allegations about his sister, who had drowned in a boating accident during a church festival-day riverside picnic at Taumarunui.

Realising that he had no legal redress against Elliot, he procured a rawhide whip and waited outside Elliot's home in Wynyard Road, Mt Eden, on the evening of 15 October. He was accompanied by his 32-year-old brother-in-law Herbert McEntee.

When Elliot came out of the house to a taxi waiting for him, Clements accused him of slandering his dead sister and proceeded to thrash him with the whip. Elliot's wife and the taxi driver tried to help him, and in the melee Elliot was punched several times in the head.

Elliot tried to escape back into his house, but his way was blocked by McEntee, and Clements continued to flail him with the whip until he thought he had had enough, at which point he released Elliot and waited for the police to arrive. He and McEntee were arrested and taken into custody but released on bail.

The next day they appeared in the Police Court where a large crowd had assembled. When the charges against them of assaulting Elliot were read out there was loud cheering, clapping and foot stomping by the audience.

The Judge ordered that the courtroom be cleared, and sometime later when the crowd had been dispersed and the case resumed, it was adjourned for a week. When the case came before the court again, the magistrate criticised Elliot for his behaviour which he described as 'a very cruel slander on the dead woman', saying that Elliot, in making his allegations in public, 'behaved like a low cad, and I am satisfied he deserved all he got and a good deal more'. He reluctantly convicted Clements but imposed no penalty, a decision that again brought cheering from the crowd in the courtroom.

# 1922

# ROMAN CATHOLIC CLERIC CHARGED WITH SEDITION

The Roman Catholic coadjutor Bishop of Auckland, James Michael Liston, kicked off a furore on 17 March 1922, when he delivered a speech to a St Patrick's Day concert in the Auckland Town Hall, condemning what he called the 'English atrocities' in Ireland.

Liston, whose position was actually the Assistant Catholic Bishop of Auckland under Bishop Cleary, had taken up his post in December 1920 after being appointed by Pope Pius XI in April of that year. He was born to Irish immigrant parents in Dunedin on 9 June 1881 and ordained in January 1904. Until his appointment to Auckland, he had been Rector of the Holy Cross College in Mosgiel. He was consecrated as coadjutor (assistant bishop) on 12 December 1920.

A crowd estimated at 2500 people gathered at the Town Hall for the annual Grand Irish Concert to mark the assumed date of death of St Patrick, the fifth-century Romano-British missionary priest who was the Bishop of Ireland and later became the patron saint of the country.

*Archbishop James Michael Liston, taken by an unidentified photographer sometime between 1929 and 1933. His statements in the Auckland Town Hall in support of Irish republicanism in 1922 caused outrage among New Zealanders loyal to the British Empire.*

Ref: 1/2-060160-F, Alexander Turnbull Library, Wellington, New Zealand

According to evidence given at the Auckland City Police Court where he was charged with seditious utterances, Liston had told the audience at the concert that his parents were driven from the country in which they were born, and would have been content to remain, by their 'foreign masters [who] did not want Irish men and women peopling their own land, but wanted to use it as a cattle ranch for the snobs of the Empire'.

> *We must not forget the martyrs who died in the fighting of 1916 — that glorious Easter. I have here a list of the men and women who were proud to die for their country. Some were shot, some were hanged, and some died on hunger strike, murdered by foreign troops. We cannot forget these men and women.*

The 'glorious Easter' he referred to was the Easter Rebellion in Dublin that began on 24 April 1916. The armed insurrection was launched by Irish republicans against British rule in Ireland with the aim of establishing an independent Irish Republic. It was the most significant rebellion in over 100 years and the first armed conflict of the Irish revolutionary period. Sixteen of the leaders were executed, but the insurrection and the aftermath contributed to an increase in support for Irish independence.

The 'foreign troops' he referred to were English soldiers.

The speech sparked an immediate response from many, including the Mayor of Auckland, James Gunson (later Sir James) who wrote to Liston the following day condemning his remarks. He also sent copies of his letter to Auckland's two daily newspapers, the *New Zealand Herald* and *The Star*.

Liston didn't reply to the points raised by Gunson in his letter — instead he wrote back to the mayor complaining that Gunson had 'issued his protest [to the press] before I could possibly have received your letter'.

> *Seeing that Your Worship had not courtesy, not to say the sense of fair play, to await my reply to your question before handing your condemnation of me to the press of New Zealand, it seems to me quite unnecessary that you should have written to me at all, and it is certainly unnecessary that I should answer your questions. As Your Worship has made this matter pubic, I am handing this letter to the press.*

Gunson also wrote to the Attorney-General and the Prime Minister with a full report of the events and raised the matter with the city solicitor to consider what action the City Council could take against Liston.

Gunson said the speech was avowedly and openly disloyal to King and country and was an affront to all New Zealand citizens.

He said it was seditious and designedly calculated to cause the 'disintegration of all that Britishers hold dear' and insulted the citizens of the Empire to which New Zealand proudly belonged. He wrote:

> *I take this first public opportunity of saying, with all the emphasis possible, that the citizens of Auckland will not tolerate for one minute such a studied and deliberate*

*Auckland's mayor, James Gunson (later Sir James) accused Liston of seditious disloyalty to King and country, and condemned his comments as 'an affront to all New Zealand citizens'.*

W.H. Bartlett via Wikimedia Commons

*act of disloyalty and of insult to British manhood and womanhood. And in making this intimation I wish to say that such a seditious and ruinous speech will not be allowed in the Auckland town hall or in any other place which the city administers, controls or licenses.*

*The Bishop and others holding views such as reported are not fit to longer enjoy the privileges and rights of a British Commonwealth and the protection of the British flag.*

His actions met with widespread support, with a steady stream of telegrams and letters arriving at the council office in support of his stand against Liston.

He was strongly supported by a wide range of people and community organisations, from the Auckland Rotary Club and the Auckland Hospital and Harbour Boards to many local bodies and the

Protestant Political Association. The Association passed a resolution congratulating Gunson on the 'loyal and patriotic manner in which he dealt with the disloyal utterances of Dr Liston'. The Welfare League complained that Liston's speech could only engender bitterness and strife among the public and 'encourage those whose efforts are directed at the destruction of the Empire'. There was limited support for Liston's views. The Hibernian Society supported him, but many prominent Roman Catholics in Auckland condemned his words.

Perhaps the editorial of *The Sun* newspaper in Christchurch summed up the feelings:

> *We suggest to Doctor Liston and others of Irish extraction that*
> *if they are not content to respect the flag that shelters them and*
> *behave as loyal citizens in New Zealand, they should return to*
> *Ireland and participate in the fray. Meanwhile the Government*
> *has a duty to perform in the matter. There is a law on the statute*
> *book regarding sedition and Doctor Liston should be taught*
> *that his rank and position do not confer upon him any special*
> *privilege to talk treason when the spirit moves him.*

On 25 March, Prime Minister William Massey (who was incidentally a Presbyterian), announced that the government had, after receiving advice from the Crown Law Office, decided to prosecute Liston on a charge of seditious utterances in connection with the speech, and the case went ahead in the Supreme Court at Auckland on Tuesday, 9 May 1922.

Opening the criminal session charge against Liston, the judge, Mr Justice Stringer, told the Grand Jury that the crime of sedition was very carefully defined in the Crimes Act while safeguarding freedom of speech and liberty of criticism.

He said under the Act, sedition was:

> *an intention to bring into hatred or contempt, or to excite*
> *disaffection against the person of His Majesty or the Government*
> *or constitution of the United Kingdom or any part thereof; or*

*to incite His Majesty's subjects to attempt to procure otherwise than by lawful means the alteration of any matter affecting the constitution, laws, or government of the United Kingdom or of New Zealand; or to raise discontent or disaffection among His Majesty's subjects; or to promote feelings of ill will and hostility between different classes of such subjects.*

Liston's speech was widely reported in the *New Zealand Herald* and *The Star*. The *New Zealand Herald* reporter Gordon Stanbrook, who had attended the concert, was called as a witness for the prosecution, producing the initial copy he wrote after the meeting, but told the court that he had disposed of the actual notes he took of Liston's speech after writing his story on the concert.

The Crown Prosecutor told the Grand Jury that the speaker of the words, by reason of his eminence in the Roman Catholic Church and the fact that he was recognised as a man of culture, learning and experience, gave his words a weight and bearing that would not be applied to a person of little or no responsibility.

After a hearing lasting two days, the all-Protestant jury retired to consider its verdict on 17 May. After less than 75 minutes of deliberation it returned a unanimous not guilty verdict on the charge of sedition, a decision greeted with an outbreak of applause from the public gallery.

The not-guilty decision came because of uncertainty over the exact words Liston had used in his speech, and because there was no proof that his speech had actually stirred up any strife in the community.

But the jury did add a unanimous rider to its finding, censuring Liston for his words:

*We consider that Dr. Liston was guilty of a grave indiscretion in using words capable of an interpretation so calculated to give offence to a large number of the public of New Zealand, and we hold that he must bear the responsibility in part at least for the unenviable notoriety that has followed his utterance.*

Liston's counsel, P.J. O'Regan and J.L. Conlan, were greeted with cheers outside the courtroom, but Liston himself had slipped quietly out through a side door.

Despite another gaffe following the December 1922 general election when he celebrated the success of the newly formed Labour Party, declaring, 'Thanks be to God — the Labour people, our friends, are coming into their own', and efforts by his boss, Bishop Cleary, to have him replaced as coadjutor, he went on to further success in the Church.

Following the death of Cleary in 1929 Liston was appointed as the seventh Bishop of Auckland, a post he held for the next 41 years, ruling in what has been called 'imperious style' and with many controversies.

Ironically, he was awarded the King George V Silver Jubilee Medal in 1935, a commemorative medal issued to mark the 25th anniversary of the ascension of King George V, and in 1968 was made a Companion of the Order of St Michael and St George (CMG).

In 1953 he was given the honorary title of Archbishop by the Church, and in 1955 was given an honorary Doctor of Laws (LLD) from the University of Auckland.

He retired from office in 1970 at the age of 88 and died in Auckland's Mater Hospital on 8 July 1976, at the age of 95.

# Scoundrels,
# Rascals
## and
# Shysters

# 1806

# NORTHLAND'S FIRST WHITE WOMEN — PIRATES OR VICTIMS?

The first white women to live in the North Island — former transported convicts Charlotte Badger and Catharine (Kitty) Hegarty — sailed into the Bay of Islands aboard the captured brig *Venus*, sometime in December 1806.

The story of how they got there reads like a movie or TV script — with drama, mystery, intrigue, romance and tragic subplots.

By the time of their arrival in the Bay of Islands Charlotte Badger was about 28 years old and Catharine Hegarty was probably a little older. They had both served time at the first Parramatta Female Factory at Port Jackson (present-day Sydney) in Australia, and both had become free women. (There are many variations of the spelling of Hegarty's name — some spell it Hagerty, others spell it Haggerty. A public notice published in the *Sydney Gazette* in July 1806 spelled the name Hegarty.)

Born in Bromsgrove, Worcestershire, Badger had been sentenced to death by the Worcester Assizes in June 1796 at the age of eighteen, after she had been found guilty of breaking into her employer's house and stealing four guineas and a Queen Anne half-crown (the equivalent of about $8.65 in total). Later her death penalty was commuted, and she was sentenced to transportation to New South Wales for seven years.

Because of the large number of convicts being shipped to New South Wales she spent the first four years of her sentence in prison in England, and it wasn't until August 1800 that she was put aboard the *Earl Cornwallis* for the voyage to Australia, along with 294 other convicts.

The voyage took 206 days and they arrived at Port Jackson on 12 June 1801, when she had just two years left of her sentence. She became a free woman on 11 June 1803.

Little is known about Catharine Hegarty. It is known that she arrived in New South Wales aboard the *Kitty* in November 1792, but her offence is unknown. Records of the convicts aboard that ship list only the names of those of English and Welsh origin. But the records also state that there were fourteen female Irish prisoners aboard, so presumably Hegarty was of Irish descent. The names Catharine and Hegarty are both Irish. Unfortunately, almost all of the official convict lists of Irish transports have been lost, so there is little or no information about any of them.

*Kitty* was formerly a slave ship transporting slaves from Africa's Gold Coast to Jamaica, and it was one of the ships making up what is now known as the 1791 Fourth Fleet, along with the *Pitt* and the *Royal Admiral*. It first left England in March 1791 with Hegarty and 29 other female convicts, ten male convicts and a cargo of stores, but it sprung a leak and had to return to Spithead for repairs. It left again in April 1792, and after stopping for more repairs in Rio de Janeiro and Cape Town, finally arrived at Port Jackson on 18 November 1792.

Sometime after her arrival, Hegarty apparently entered into a relationship with Port Jackson's controversial Judge-Advocate Richard Atkins, who was by all accounts a highly disreputable and dishonourable character. She was living with him, and he is known to have been the father of at least one of her children, a son.

He gave Hegarty a full pardon in 1800 and that same year she returned to London, taking their son with her, but in 1803 her son returned to New South Wales to live with his father. Hegarty returned at some stage, but it's not known if she came back with her son, or if she returned sometime later. She was certainly back there by June 1806 when the *Venus* drama began.

At some point, her relationship with Atkins had ended, and she began a relationship with an American whaler by the name of Benjamin Burnet Kelly who was the first mate of the *Venus* and who had arrived in Australia aboard the whaling ship *Albion*. The *Albion* worked around New Zealand and Australia, and in 1803 took convicts, free settlers and officials from England to Risdon Cove, Van Diemen's Land, now known as Tasmania, where a new settlement was to be established.

In 1806, the colonial government chartered the *Venus* to carry supplies to another penal colony at Port Dalrymple located on the Tamar River on the north coast of Van Diemen's Land. The *Venus* was a 45-ton brigantine that had been built in Calcutta for the Port Jackson merchant Robert Campbell & Co, and it had arrived at Port Jackson on 8 May 1805.

The vessel left for Port Dalrymple on 29 April under the command of Captain Rodman Chace, with a cargo of salted pork and other supplies for the settlement.

The complement included two convicts, Thomas Evans and John Lancaster or Lancashire. Lancaster was described in official notifications of the time as 'a very dangerous person' and 'a big truculent-looking man' and Chace had reluctantly agreed to convey him to Port Dalrymple.

Also aboard were Kitty Hegarty who was sharing the cabin of Benjamin Kelly, and for unknown reasons, Charlotte Badger was also aboard along with her infant child, believed to have been a daughter named Ann. One report suggests that she was there as the partner of convict John Lancaster. Another suggests that both women, having served their sentences and now being free women, were being sent to Van Diemen's Land to take up roles as house servants.

An official record of 1806 described Badger as a very corpulent person with a full face, thick lips and light hair, and with an infant in arms. Hegarty is described as a very handsome woman with white teeth, a fresh complexion and 'much inclined to smile and a great talker'. En route to Dalrymple the ship put into Twofold Bay on the coast of New South Wales, about 550 kilometres south of Port Jackson, where it was delayed for about a month by contrary winds, and that was where things started to go wrong.

One day Captain Chace went ashore and, on his return to the *Venus* about dusk, he was greeted with a rowdy drunken party. During his absence some of the crew and the convicts had broken into the hold and had helped themselves to stores of rum.

Chace later said that Badger and Hegarty were entertaining the menfolk, dancing to the accompaniment of violin music provided by the cook, an earless Malaysian named Darra, while Kelly dished out the rum. Other crewmen and convicts were lying on the deck in various stages of drunkenness.

The captain brought the party to an end, throwing the rum overboard, and clapping irons on the drunks. Kelly confronted Chace with 'a Bowie knife of alarming dimensions' challenging the captain to a fight, but he backed down when Chace threatened him with a pistol.

With relative order restored and a favourable wind at last, the *Venus* resumed its voyage to Van Diemen's Land until Chace learned that during the drunken revelry Hegarty had thrown overboard a wooden box which contained papers that he was to deliver to the commander at Port Dalrymple. Why she did so is unknown.

The ship was put about and returned to Twofold Bay to search for the box but was unsuccessful and the voyage was resumed.

On 16 June 1806, they arrived at their destination and Captain Chace went ashore to meet with the commander, Lieutenant House, and report on the difficulties he had experienced. He planned to stay the night ashore and had ordered the crew to up-anchor at six o'clock the next morning and sail up the Tamar River to meet him at Port Dalrymple, where the supplies could be unloaded.

About seven o'clock the next morning, Chace and House were heading towards the *Venus* in a longboat when they saw the ship get under way. They landed at a nearby bay to wait for the ship to arrive,

*Port Dalrymple as it appeared in 1808, two years after the* Venus *mutiny.*
Courtesy of Mitchell Library, State Library of New South Wales

but about an hour later there was no sign of the *Venus*. Instead they saw another longboat heading towards them from downriver, rowed by five exhausted and bleeding men.

They told Chace that just after the ship had got under way, Kelly, the two convicts Evans and Lancaster, the pilot David Evans, the soldier Corporal Richard Thompson, Darra the cook, and the two women, all armed with pistols and swords, had seized control of the ship and ordered them into the longboat.

They said that Kelly, with his arm around Hegarty, called out to them to pass on his compliments to Captain Chace, Lieutenant House and the Lieutenant-Governor, and let them know that they were planning a South Pacific cruise. They then set sail downriver towards the open sea with the cargo of supplies still on board, including many personal possessions of the Van Diemen's Land settlers. The loss of the government's supplies was put at £460 ($920). The value of the personal property still on board is unknown.

What remains unclear is whether Badger and Hegarty were willing and active participants in the mutiny, or whether they were dragged along by their partners, Kelly and Lancaster. Both situations have been suggested for the two women.

When news of the capture of the ship reached Port Jackson, the Governor issued an official proclamation asking 'all governors and officers in command at any of His Majesty's ports, and the Honourable East India Company's magistrates or officers in command, at home or abroad, at whatever port the said brig may be taken into, or met with at sea, against any frauds or deceptions that may be practised by the offending parties' to seize the pirates so they might be brought to justice.

Despite their relative inexperience as sailors, the mutineers managed to sail the *Venus* across the Tasman, arriving in New Zealand some weeks later.

Accounts vary of what happened here, but from this point the story takes a dramatic and tragic turn.

One version is that they made landfall somewhere in the North Cape region, where they came across the local Te Aupōuri people. This version says the mutineers kidnapped two high-ranking Te Aupōuri women who they apparently used as sex slaves, before fleeing to Rangihoua Bay in the Bay of Islands, about 10 kilometres north of Paihia, where they arrived in mid-December.

Another version is that the mutineers went directly to the Bay of Islands, but agreeing that they were there by mid-December 1806, and that was where the kidnappings took place.

Perhaps relationships aboard had become strained or some of the mutineers thought they would be safe in distant, isolated, lawless New Zealand, because Kelly and Badger and her child, Lancaster and Hegarty, and one of the *Venus*' two cabin boys, Thomas Ford (aged fourteen) or William Evans (aged sixteen), left the ship at Rangihoua Bay and settled on land.

Again, there are varying accounts of what happened to them. Charlotte Badger and Catharine Hegarty are said to have lived in huts on the shores of the bay under the protection of Ngāpuhi, but that both had been declared tapu. Another source says Badger was involved in a relationship with a local Māori chief. There is little evidence to support this.

Shortly after their arrival, however, Hegarty died, which must have been early in 1807. There is some suggestion that she was in fact murdered by a jealous Māori wahine while Kelly was away and was quickly buried. It appears that Badger and her daughter were taken aboard the whale ship *Indispensable* under Captain Robert Turnbull in the Bay of Islands in April that year, and they were taken to Norfolk Island where they arrived in June 1807.

From there, they sailed to Port Jackson aboard the government brig HMS *Porpoise*, arriving there on 13 July 1807. On 4 June 1811, she married Thomas Humphries, a British soldier, and the couple apparently had a daughter in 1815 whom they named Maria. Thomas Humphries died in December 1843.

Charlotte Badger was last recorded in an 1825 census, and after that she vanishes from history.

Meanwhile, the mutineers were heading into deep trouble with tragic consequences. After depositing the castaways, the mutineers kidnapped two high-ranking Ngāpuhi rangatira wahine and fled before the locals could react. One of the kidnapped women was the sister of Te Morenga, one of the most powerful chiefs in the Bay of Islands at the time, and the other was related to another famous and ferocious chief, Hongi Hika.

They stopped off at Whangārei where once more two high-born women were kidnapped, one of them Tawaputa, the niece of Te Morenga, and the ship sailed off towards the Hauraki Gulf and present-day Thames.

Accounts vary about what happened there. Some suggest that the ship was visited by the local Ngāti Pāoa chief Te Haupa and his daughter, at which point the ship set sail with them aboard. According to this version, Te Haupa leapt overboard and was picked up by a chasing canoe. Another report says the pair were among a number of Māori kidnapped by the mutineers, but that Te Haupa managed to escape the captors and leapt overboard, but the others remained as prisoners.

From there, *Venus* sailed into the Bay of Plenty, stopping at Mōtītī Island, 12 kilometres off present-day Pāpāmoa Beach, where they sold Tawaputa as a slave wife to Hukere, a Ngāi Tauwhao chief. Exactly what happened next is unclear, but there was some dispute between Hukere and another chief, Te Waru — the leading chief of Ngāi Te Rangi — over Tawaputa, and the outcome was that she was killed by Te Waru and subsequently cooked and eaten.

Some of the other kidnapped women were also sold off as slaves and met the same fate in other parts of the Bay of Plenty and East Cape areas, including Te Morenga's sister, who was killed and eaten by Ngāti Porou at Kawakawa Bay near East Cape.

News of the fate of the women eventually reached Northland where Te Morenga and Hongi Hika gathered muskets and powder, and in 1818 set out for the Bay of Plenty to seek utu.

Te Morenga led a fleet of Ngāpuhi waka taua (war canoes) south and attacked Ngāi Tauwhao at their Matarehua Pā at Taumaihi, a small islet just south of Mōtītī Island. The locals, being armed only with traditional weapons, were no match for the northerners and their muskets, and there was awful slaughter. Hundreds were captured and taken back to Northland as slaves, including the wife of Hukere. Hukere himself was killed in the slaughter, but Te Waru managed to escape and fled to the mainland.

Utu wasn't satisfied, however, and two years later in January 1820, Te Morenga once again led a war party to the area, this time to present-day Tauranga where Te Waru had sought shelter among his Ngāi Te Rangi tribesmen.

In the ensuing battles, almost 400 Ngāi Te Rangi were killed and about 200 others were captured and taken back to the Bay of Islands as slaves. Te Morenga also seized all Te Waru's canoes and took the tattooed heads of a number of Ngāi Te Rangi chiefs. Te Waru's father was one of the fatalities, but Te Waru himself escaped and later met and made peace with Te Morenga, utu having been fulfilled.

What became of Lancaster and Kelly, and what happened to the *Venus* and its remaining occupants after Mōtītī Island, is a mystery.

Some accounts say that Kelly was captured by a Royal Navy ship in 1808 and was taken back to England where he was hanged for piracy.

There is a story that his cohort Lancaster was also captured, this time by the American whaling ship *The Brothers*, and taken to Sydney where he was hanged. There is no record of a whaling ship called *The Brothers*. There was an American whaler named *Two Brothers*, but there is no record that it ever operated in New Zealand waters, and it was wrecked near Hawaii in 1823.

The consensus is that most of them probably fell victim to vengeful Māori seeking utu for the outrages they were responsible for over the deaths of the kidnapped Māori women.

The fate of the *Venus* is also unknown, but there is one story that the ship was run aground in the Bay of Plenty or around East Cape by Māori, stripped of all its valuables and set alight so that its metal nails and screws could be recovered.

The story of Badger and Hegarty inspired several works of popular culture fiction in the later nineteenth and early twentieth centuries, many of which sensationalised and dramatised their experiences, and that has resulted in their stories being badly distorted. Various writers, authors and even playwrights, musical producers and radio dramatists have portrayed them as wanton, willing pirates, sometimes even as the ringleaders of the *Venus* mutiny plot.

Current knowledge about their sad lives tends to discredit these claims, and while they were probably not complete innocents, nor were they the women portrayed in popular fiction.

Rather it seems they were victims of their era and the unscrupulous men they became involved with.

# 1827

# THE CONVICT MUTINEERS

In Britain in the seventeenth and eighteenth centuries, even the most minor crimes could see you facing the death sentence or banished to the furthest reaches of the earth, usually under brutal administrations managed by sadistic, cruel tyrants, a punishment that the convicted often took extreme measures to avoid.

Britain began exporting its criminals to the New World, initially the American colonies, in 1610 and over the next 166 years, an estimated 50,000 convicts — mostly men — were sent to America, usually to the Chesapeake Colonies of Maryland and Virginia.

But that came to an end at the outbreak of the American War of Independence in 1776, and nine years later, with British prisons running out of space to house its burgeoning prison population, the English turned to Australia as a location for penal settlements, and in May 1787 the First Fleet of eleven convict ships set sail for Botany Bay with some 800 convicts aboard.

Over the next few decades, it created penal settlements in New South Wales, Tasmania, Queensland and Western Australia, and in 1788, Norfolk Island. The island was one of the most brutal settlements that was designed to accommodate the very worst offenders and had a fearsome reputation for harsh and inhumane treatment.

In December 1826, the brig *Wellington* — under the command of Captain John Harwood — set sail from Sydney bound for Norfolk Island with its complement of 66 male prisoners along with twelve soldiers and a sergeant whose job it was to guard the prisoners on the voyage, and two other passengers.

The *Wellington* had been chartered by the British Government to transport the convicts and their guards, along with stores for the re-established Norfolk Island penal settlement which had reopened in 1824 after closing in 1814 because of the difficulty and expense of getting supplies to the settlement. All went according to plan for eleven days. But on 21 December, when the ship was about 400 kilometres from Norfolk Island, the prisoners seized control.

This happened about noon when six prisoners who were exercising on the deck turned on their two armed guards and overpowered them, seizing their muskets. The soldiers were locked in the forecastle of the ship and another 40 prisoners were freed, then some of the crew was rounded up and locked in the prison hold, along with about 20 convicts who wanted no part of the mutiny.

While the soldiers were securely locked in the forecastle they were still armed with the muskets, and they fired on the mutineers through the bulkhead. That stopped, however, after they were told that all they were doing was endangering the crewmen who were working the ship. They were then stripped of their weapons and their uniforms, which the mutineers then dressed themselves in.

At this point one of the passengers — William Buchanan — emerged from his cabin brandishing two pistols, but his efforts ended when he was struck down by a blow to the head with the butt of a musket. At this point the mutineers had complete control of the ship, which they celebrated by breaking out the store of wines and spirits. The takeover had been completed with no loss of life and only some minor bullet wounds, cuts and bruises.

The celebrations were short-lived, however, as a storm struck in the evening and the mutineers had to call on the imprisoned crew to help man the ship.

They were a largely disciplined mob and quickly created a command structure with John Walton — a former subaltern with the 48th Regiment who had been transported on a charge of receiving stolen property — appointed captain. He was assisted by a council of seven others who were charged with implementing a system of keeping the peace and controlling supplies such as water and food. They set up a democratic system where decisions were made by majority vote and no one had any more say or control than any other, and they drew up a list of rules to create a far more egalitarian system than normally applied on sailing ships at the time.

The *Wellington*'s council was kept busy with two major decisions — first, to decide their ultimate destination and, second, what to do with their unwanted passengers.

They knew that Britain was persistent in hunting down escapers and making an example of them. In 1808, 50 convicts had seized control of the brig *Harrington* and fled to the South China Sea, but they were recaptured and returned to Sydney where the ringleaders were hanged.

The mutineers' decision was to offload their captives and then head for South America, but it was clear that they didn't have sufficient supplies, mainly fresh water, for such a lengthy voyage, so the decision was made to head for New Zealand to resupply the ship and offload their prisoners. The Manawatāwhi Three Kings Islands off the northern tip of New Zealand were chosen for this purpose, but after being told that their captives might fall victim to cannibalism if they were abandoned on the islands, they changed that for the Bay of Islands where missionaries would provide protection.

Captain Harwood was freed so he could navigate the *Wellington* to the Bay of Islands.

Surviving records from John Walton's meticulously kept daily log and transcripts from the eventual trial of the mutineers show that conditions aboard were peaceful and harmonious, and that discipline was maintained justly. Christmas Day was celebrated with a feast and extra wine and spirits, and maintenance and cleanliness of the ship continued as usual. The weather was kind to the mutineers as well — they recorded only one day becalmed and one day when a severe thunderstorm struck.

Finally on New Year's Day — 1 January 1827 — the west coast of New

Zealand was sighted, and four days later, on 5 January, the *Wellington* sailed into the Bay of Islands — and their plans started to unravel.

At that time the Bay of Islands was a busy place. A favourable climate, rich soil and an abundance of fish had attracted a sizeable indigenous population, factors which in turn attracted Church Missionary Society (CMS) missionaries to the area. The addition of an excellent harbour meant that it was also a very popular place for whaling ships to berth. The main European settlement, Kororāreka (now Russell), was an important trading and supply centre but — despite the best efforts of the Christian missionaries — it was a rugged and lawless town with a rough and tough population, earning it the reputation of 'the hell hole of the South Pacific'.

About eight o'clock in the morning of 5 January the *Wellington* arrived off the settlement near two whaling ships, the Australian-owned and operated *Sisters*, under the command of Captain Robert Duke, and the British-owned *Harriet*, commanded by Captain John Clark. Her arrival was also noted by the Reverend Henry Williams, the superintendent of the CMS mission station at Paihia.

Captains Duke and Clark both went to offer their assistance to the *Wellington*, which was accepted, and they boarded to help bring the

*Kororāreka as it appeared in 1835, eight years after the* Wellington *visit to the Bay of Islands. This aquatint is by the London-born artist Joel Samuel Polack, who built a substantial home at the north end of the beach.*
Ref: PUBL-0115-1-front, Alexander Turnbull Library, Wellington, New Zealand

ship to anchor. Once aboard they met 'Commander' Walton who told them the ship was from Sydney and was en route to 'the River Thames' (Coromandel) with supplies and troops but was in need of fresh water, hence their arrival in the Bay of Islands.

Both Duke and Clark were surprised that more water was needed after such a short voyage and at the unprofessional manner in which the ship was being handled, but neither was suspicious about the situation, and they returned to their own vessels.

Later that day missionary William Fairburn called on Duke to ask if the *Wellington* was carrying any mail for the mission station. Both men then rowed over to the brig to find out, and that's when things started to go wrong: *Wellington* was swarming with Māori visitors who were on the deck and in the rigging, and particularly below deck, where there were many women enjoying wine and beer. Their suspicions deepened when Fairburn recognised one of the 'crew' as a convict who had been a painter in Sydney, and Duke recognised another of the 'crew' as someone who had been condemned to Norfolk Island.

But saying nothing, they departed back to *Sisters* to discuss the situation, and decided to invite 'Commander' Walton to join them for dinner aboard

*The Rev. Henry Williams of the CMS station at Paihia who recorded the entry of the* Wellington *to the Bay of Islands on the morning of 5 January 1827. From a painting by Charles Baugniet about 1854.*

Ref: C-020-005, Alexander Turnbull Library, Wellington, New Zealand

the ship. Walton declined the invitation but said he would join them for an hour later in the afternoon. When he failed to appear, Duke, Clark, Fairburn and Williams rowed back across to *Wellington* where they found a party well under way, which along with the large amount of water being loaded aboard — far more than would be necessary for a voyage to the Firth of Thames — confirmed their suspicions.

The invitation to Walton to join them for dinner was issued again and this time accepted, and as the four men left the *Wellington*, someone secretly slipped a note to Fairburn which turned out to be from Captain Harwood, the *Wellington*'s real captain, detailing what had happened.

Walton duly arrived for dinner where he was questioned more closely by his hosts and the note shown to him, at which point he admitted the truth, telling his interrogators that they planned to sail to South America.

Duke, Clark, Williams and Fairburn told Walton that they were holding him prisoner and would not let him leave the *Sisters*. But later that night for some unknown reason they relented and let him return to the *Wellington*. Williams, who had served as a British Navy lieutenant during the Napoleonic Wars, urged Duke to fire his cannons at the *Wellington* in an attempt to disable the ship, but the others rejected that, worried that the mutineers might retaliate or that their captives might be harmed.

The following day — a Saturday — Duke lined up his eight cannons on the *Wellington* in case of an attack, but at eight o'clock the *Wellington* drew alongside the *Harriet*, seeking to trade some of the government-owned equipment they had aboard for supplies for the voyage to South America, an offer that was declined. However, Clark and Duke did accept an invitation from Walton to board the *Wellington*, during which time they were able to talk to the hostages, learning that they had been well-treated. At the same time, a document was drawn up exonerating Captain Harwood and the crew from any complicity in the seizure of the ship.

Despite the fact that the mutineers had the necessary firepower and numbers to win any fight against the whaling ships and having the opportunity to imprison both captains which would have left the whalers leaderless, Walton let both Duke and Clark return to their ships.

At 4 a.m. the next day preparations were under way aboard the *Wellington* to depart on the voyage to South America, but at 5 a.m. both the *Sisters* and the *Harriet* — which was armed with six long cannons — opened fire on the ship, damaging the masts, the rigging and the hull. Despite their superior firepower and numbers, the mutineers offered no defence against the attack, with many leaping overboard to escape the bombardment and others fleeing below decks, before signalling their surrender.

Negotiations then began between the mutineers and Duke, Clark, Williams and Fairburn and it was agreed that the mutineers could go ashore, which they were reluctant to do 'until the natives had dispersed', fearing that they might be eaten. When the Māori had dispersed at the request of Williams and Fairburn, the mutineers went ashore, leaving the *Wellington*'s crew, and those who had not taken part in the mutiny, on board.

Their problems weren't over, however, because once they were onshore, the Māori returned to plunder their belongings, and the mutineers fled into the bush in panic, where they became separated. Williams arranged with local Māori to hunt down the escapees, a task which took more than two weeks, and even then it wasn't completely successful, with six mutineers never seen again. What became of them is lost to history.

Not so the rest. They were held captive aboard the three ships where they made a number of unsuccessful escape attempts, and once repairs had been made to the *Wellington*, she and the *Sisters* departed for Sydney on 28 January 1827 with the surviving mutineers. They arrived there on 9 February, an event that was met with the nineteenth-century version of a media frenzy.

Sydney newspapers seemingly couldn't get enough of the story of the mutiny, devoting huge coverage to it and exploring every angle. Then attention shifted to the more serious issue of the consequences, which presented Australia's colonial administration with something of a dilemma. Public opinion was largely sympathetic to the mutineers in view of the kindness and consideration that they had shown to the crew and military contingent of the *Wellington*.

According to the letter of the law of the time, hanging was the punishment for mutiny, but hanging all 40 mutineers would have caused outrage in the community so authorities decided on a compromise: those who had originally been sentenced to death in Britain, but whose sentences had been commuted to transportation, would be hanged. The reasoning was that they had abused the mercy that had been shown to them by commuting their sentences.

That meant that six were sentenced to hang: William Douglass, John Edwards, James Smith, Edward Colthurst, Richard Johnson and William Leddington. The apparent ringleader — former soldier John Walton — escaped the noose because his original crime, receiving stolen property, wasn't a capital offence, was his first offence and because of the good conduct and humanity he had shown to his prisoners on board *Wellington*. Instead, he was sentenced to life with hard labour on Norfolk Island. William Douglass also escaped the hangman, after the soldiers and Sergeant of the Guard on board the *Wellington* petitioned for mercy because he had saved their lives during the takeover of the ship.

The five others were duly hanged in a public spectacle at The Rocks on 12 March 1827 where a large crowd had gathered to watch, apparently not completely happy at the justice that was being carried out. The Sydney newspaper, *The Australian*, recorded:

> *A general impulse of regret that their previous actions should have called for this awful sacrifice, appeared to pervade the minds of the spectators generally.*

Another newspaper, *The Monitor*, noted:

> *. . .this execution [was] the most dismal, heart-rending sight of the kind we ever before witnessed.*

Between the start of shipments in 1788 and the end of the system in 1868, Britain sent 162,000 convicts to Australia, about 23,000 of them were women. A good number of them or their descendants moved on to New Zealand, perhaps to escape the dark shadow of their convict heritage.

# 1857

# THE SHIPWRECK THAT WASN'T

In colonial Collingwood in Mōhua Golden Bay, a straggling band of bearded and half-starved men made their way to the Resident Magistrate on 9 September 1857, with an extraordinary tale of shipwreck, struggle and survival.

The five men, led by a seaman calling himself Theodore Jerome, told the Resident Magistrate Henry G. Gouland that they were survivors of the shipwreck of the US-whaling barque *Pacific*, a 350-ton sailing ship owned by Swift and Perry of New Bedford, which he claimed sank at Milford Haven — now Piopiotahi Milford Sound — on 21 May 1857. The barque had a complement of about 32, meaning that some 24 men had supposedly lost their lives in the shipwreck.

In a sworn deposition, Jerome said the *Pacific* had left New Bedford in June 1856 on a twelve-month whaling voyage and had put in to 'Bunberry in New Holland' (actually Bunbury in Western Australia) for supplies and caulking in January 1857 before heading to Milford Haven. He claimed the ship 'leaked considerably'. At that time the seas off Milford Sound and west of Foveaux Strait were prime whaling grounds. One recent report identified 187 vessels that hunted in the area at that time.

*Whaling as it was carried out in 1857 at the time of the* Pacific *hoax. From an illustration in the 1855 book* Timboo and Joliba — The Art of Being Useful.
Internet Archive Book Images, via Wikimedia Commons

Jerome told the magistrate that the ship reached New Zealand in February and was whaling off the coast when it was hit by several gales, which increased the leakage considerably. The crew manned the pumps continuously into the night, but the leaks continued to increase, which led to the ship's carpenter declaring the vessel to be dangerous and the captain deciding to abandon her.

Jerome's statement claimed the captain ordered everyone into the boats about 11.30 p.m., and the boat he was in was lowered about half an hour later, even though heavy seas were washing over the ship and it was settling by the stern. He claimed he saw one other boat being lowered. His boat landed about 3.30 a.m. 'between Milford Cove and Open Bay on the Milford Haven side of Cascade Point', but he said it had been wrecked on the shoreline. According to his account, his was the only lifeboat to make it to shore.

Next morning the survivors scanned the coastline but saw no trace of the *Pacific* or any of the lifeboats.

According to him, eight crewmen had made it to shore and after resting for a day, they tried to head south but were prevented because of the thick bush. They then headed north towards Open Bay Island just south of Haast, where they claimed they met a party of Māori sealers. They spent about two weeks at the bay before seven of them headed north again, using directions given to them by one of the Māori who could speak a little English. They left behind a boy aged about sixteen at Open Bay, apparently because he had problems with his feet and couldn't make the walk.

Three months later five crewmen managed to make their way to Collingwood: two others reportedly remained at Māori settlements along the way. Jerome claimed that the Māori they met on their trek were very kind to them, giving them food and enabling them to stay alive to reach the settlement.

Jerome's statements were verified by the other four in the party. But it seems that it was all a fabrication, and in fact the supposed survivors were deserters who escaped from the ship at Milford Sound and, along with deserters from other whaling ships, made their way north to Golden Bay.

This is probably correct as there is a record of a whaling ship called *Pacific* from New Bedford returning to Hobart in 1858 with a cargo of 100 barrels of sperm oil from whales caught off South Westland, at that time valued at about £8000.

Records of the *Pacific's* log indicate they experienced difficult weather for the four months they spent off South Westland, spending 58 days sheltering from bad weather and about another 25 days unable to chase whales because of fog. The log reports that several ships in Milford Haven had lost crew through desertion, and that five crew had stolen a boat from the *Pacific* and disappeared while the ship was anchored in Milford Sound.

Somehow Magistrate Gouland became aware of the deception, because two years later in September 1857, he wrote to *The Nelson Examiner* expressing his belief that it was all a hoax. He said:

> THE WHALING BARQUE PACIFIC.
> *Sir — I have reason to believe that the deposition of the man who*
> *called himself Theodore Jerome, respecting the supposed loss of*

*the American barque Pacific on the west coast of this island, was, so far as respects the danger of the vessel, a fabrication.*

Gouland said that although he had not been able to procure evidence on the subject, he had every reason to believe that the men were deserters from the ship, and that they escaped in a boat at Milford Haven, and he asked the editor of the *Nelson Examiner* — and other newspapers that had run the original report — to publish his letter to set the record straight in case 'Jerome's deposition may cause uneasiness to the owners of the vessel and the relations of the people on board'. Further light is thrown on the hoax by the autobiography *Four Years Aboard a Whaleship*, written in 1864 by W.B. Whitecar, in which he dismisses Jerome's claims as 'a tissue of falsehoods fabricated by deserters from the ship'.

He says there is 'not a particle of truth' in the sworn affidavit: the ship never leaked seriously during the voyage, only requiring to be pumped once a week to keep under control, and the carpenter mentioned in the affidavit never existed.

Whitecar says the hoax was conceived by a deserter named Joseph Riley, a native of New Jersey of Irish extraction, who was an experienced seaman, hence he was able to concoct a believable hoax, while Theodore Jerome is likely to have been John Roberts, a London cockney who had been transported to Australia. Roberts had sailed on the *Henry H Crapo*, a Dartmouth-built sailing ship named after its part-owner, a Massachusetts businessman and civic leader, but he left her in Western Australia when he joined the *Pacific*.

There actually was a seaman on board the *Pacific* named Theodore Jerome and he was said to be 'justly indignant at the liberties taken in his name'. Roberts had in his possession an American protection document in the name of Jerome which he had apparently stolen. Whitecar records that Roberts was 'weak-minded with little intelligence, and totally incapable of giving such an account, except at the instigation of a person like Riley, and afterwards being well drilled until he was perfect in his part'. Records show some of the deserters — William Harvey Millar, Joseph Riley, William C. Bayles and David Jones — had been part of the *Pacific* crew, while William (or John) Owen, William Anderson and David Ling were the names of deserters from the barque *Lady Emma*, who had joined the *Pacific* deserters at Open Bay Island.

As far as is known Miller and Ling never arrived in Collingwood, and what became of Roberts and Riley and their co-conspirators is not recorded by history.

Concocting the shipwreck story meant they were sympathetically received by the Collingwood community whereas had it been known that they were in fact deserters, their reception would have been a lot different!

Desertions were not uncommon from whaling ships because of the terrible conditions the crews lived under and the minimal payment they received, which was calculated as a share of the earnings from the sale of the harvest. That varied from a 1/16th share for the first officer down to a 1/65th share for a seaman, which for them meant a payment of about £24 for up to two years' work.

# 1866

# A DUFFER OF A RUSH

Gold fever was rampant on the West Coast in the 1860s, and at the centre of the excitement was a shadowy prospector by the name of Albert Hunt, remembered as the instigator of the Bruce Bay duffer gold rush.

Hunt claimed credit for the Coast's first payable gold strike at Greenstone Creek, and later proclaimed that he made another discovery at Bruce Bay, about halfway between Haast and Fox Glacier in South Westland.

Finding payable goldfields was something of a fixation with New Zealand's early provincial governments. Following the discovery of gold at Gabriel's Gully in the Otago Province in 1861, the Canterbury Provincial Council offered a reward of £1000 ($2000) to anyone who found gold in payable quantities in the Canterbury province. The reward was a very sizeable enticement in the 1860s — by twenty-first century values, it was worth about $2 million.

At that time, Canterbury incorporated West Canterbury, known today as the West Coast.

Hunt's claim that he had found gold at Greenstone Creek, a tributary of the Taramakau River near Kumara in 1864, led to the Coast's first gold rush.

Other sources say that Hunt didn't find the Greenstone Creek gold at all, but that it had been discovered by two Māori prospectors, Ihaia Tainui (also known as Samuel) and Haimona Taukau (also known as Simon) in 1862. Taukau had apparently also found gold in Lyell Creek, a tributary of the Buller River, also in 1862.

According to an account written in the 1860s by West Coast prospector and store owner, Reuben Waite, Hunt did not discover gold himself, but was led to it by Tainui and Taukau. Another writer of the times, prospector William Martin, provides more information: he wrote that Simon and Samuel had found gold while searching for pounamu in Greenstone Creek, a tributary of the Taramakau River. (Greenstone Creek later became known as the Greenstone River or the Big Hohonu River. In 1998 under the Ngāi Tahu Claims Settlement Act its name officially became the Greenstone River/Hokonui.)

Martin wrote that Hunt had been idling for months in the Māori settlement and that 'out of good nature, Simon and his mate disclosed their find directly to him, and directed him where to go'. They gave him a lift in their canoe 'to the Hohuna [sic] where Tainui and Taukau each had a whare. It was an easy day's walk from there to the Greenstone.' In 1865 Hunt attempted to collect the £1000 reward offered by the Canterbury Provincial Council for the discovery of a paying goldfield, even though the offer had been withdrawn in 1863, a year before Hunt's claimed Greenstone Creek discovery.

His attempt to claim the reward led to heated debate among Council members. Some said Hunt had no legal claim to the reward, others tried to organise the payment of a lesser amount in recognition of his service rendered to the province. Finally, a vote was taken on a proposal to pay him £250, a motion that was soundly rejected by the Council in a nineteen to four vote. Nevertheless, a payment of £200 was eventually made to him as a gratuity in recognition of his services in exploring and developing the province's resources.

Despite that rejection, Hunt was generally recognised as the man responsible for the discovery of the Greenstone Creek goldfield, and in 1866 he applied for and was granted a claim six miles (10 km) south of and nine miles (15 km) inland from Bruce Bay, about halfway between present day Haast and Fox Glacier.

At the time he was based in Ōkārito, 62 miles (100 km) north of Bruce Bay, which was then one of the largest towns on the Coast, because of the nearby goldfield. The town had sprung up at the south end of Ōkārito lagoon, the entrance to which was a main shipping channel for ships into the port of Ōkārito. It was the third largest port on the Coast at that time and continued to operate until the 1940s.

During the 1860s, hundreds of miners from all over the world landed there. By 1866, the town had 33 stores and a population of more than 4000 people. In 1865 it was estimated that there were more than 16,000 prospectors working along the Coast.

Because of Hunt's reputation as the discoverer of the Greenstone Creek goldfield, everyone was keeping a close eye on his movements, hoping he would lead them to his new goldfield.

Such was Hunt's reputation that once he was granted the concession to his Bruce Bay claim and the locality of the claim described, hundreds set off in search of it. It seems some were desperate to follow any lead, however slim, in the hope of striking it rich.

Early on the afternoon of 21 March 1866, Hunt arrived at Bruce Bay

*Ōkārito township, as it appeared about 1946.*
National Publicity Studios, New Zealand Government, via Wikimedia Commons

surrounded by a 'very formidable bodyguard', and he was immediately mobbed by an estimated 500 miners who had been waiting for him. He managed to make his way to a local store for supplies, after which he agreed to lead the miners to the new field and to set out immediately, despite the lateness of the hour.

The first difficulty they faced was a bluff at the south end of Bruce Bay. They had to clamber over that which, according to a report of that time, was 'most difficult' because of the numbers pushing their way through afraid that they might lose sight of Hunt in the lead.

Five miles further on, the entourage, now numbering an estimated 1500 people, came to what was referred to as the Pukiriki River (probably the Paringa River) which they crossed immediately, setting up camp for the night on the other side.

The next morning, the eager miners were up early to keep an eye on their guide, and after breakfast they began their trek.

The conditions being tough, many decided to split up, leaving some behind with their supplies, so others, freed of heavy burden, could make fast time to the supposed claim.

They set off along the coast until unexpectedly Hunt took a sudden turn and disappeared into thick bush.

There was a mad rush by the hundreds of trailing miners in an endeavour to follow him, with many ending up stuck in the bush and others tumbling down crevasses. Many did manage to continue to trail Hunt, however, although the pace was such that after some five miles some were too exhausted to go on and collapsed along the track.

The chase continued for another three or four miles before everyone halted for a rest and a drink of water from a stream before continuing, this time in heavy rain, for another couple of miles before the followers realised that Hunt had given them the slip.

They waited, some in the hope that Hunt would realise they weren't behind him and would return to get them, but of course he didn't.

Night fell along with heavy rain, but few had any shelter or food, having left all that behind at Pukiriki River. They spent a very cold and uncomfortable night in the open.

Newspaper eyewitness reports from the time said after braving the storm and heavy rain of the night, in the morning 'curses and threats of vengeance on Hunt were heard in all directions'.

But it wasn't the end of Hunt — a few days later, he accidentally stumbled into some of those he had deceived, apparently while he was trying to escape the area. He was quickly captured and taken to the miners' camp where he agreed to their demands to take them to his gold find.

For half a day he led them through the bush until they set up an overnight camp at Granite Creek. Early next morning, Hunt told them he had to climb a tree to make sure of his bearings, which he did while the rest broke camp. But when they were ready to depart, they were astounded to find that Hunt had once again vanished.

They scoured the surrounding bush but could find no trace of him. One prospector reportedly did see him late in the evening but was unable to capture him, Hunt escaping without his hat and shirt.

Realising their expedition was over, most of the men returned to Bruce Bay, leaving a couple of hundred men behind at Granite Creek, to prospect the area. That evening there were reportedly two to three thousand men camping on the beach at the Bruce Bay settlement of Weld and threatening dire vengeance on Hunt for his deception, if they could locate him. Many waited around for a day or two just in case Hunt should reappear, or that there might be news of the exact location of his gold claim. But there were no further sightings of Hunt on the Coast, and no trace of his supposed gold find.

Just what was the motive behind Hunt's deception is unknown. Some believed he was exacting revenge for the way the miners had treated him earlier over the Greenstone Creek goldfield find, while others believed he had genuinely become lost in the thick bush. That is considered unlikely because Hunt was an experienced bushman who had been born and bred in the bush.

Hunt's brother had apparently also been taken in by the hoax and had joined the march into the bush. His name was William Albert Hunt, and he was credited with the later discovery of the Shotover quartz goldfield at Thames on the Coromandel in 1867.

He later told authorities that he believed his brother's Bruce Bay rush was a 'complete humbug'.

Feelings were running hot among some of the prospectors and in Weld on Friday, 30 March, tempers boiled over with 30 to 40 miners, apparently the worse for wear after drinking heavily, rioting in the town, breaking into stores and stealing liquor and supplies.

The first to be hit was the store of Ecclefield Brothers where food and liquor were taken and the building damaged. Next was the store of Brennan & Byrnes where whole cases of brandy and port were taken. The worst affected was the store of Smith and Wood, where liquor and goods to the value of £200 ($400) were taken. Altogether the stores reported losses of £664 ($1328), and six stores were virtually destroyed.

Other stores and shanties were also broken into and goods stolen.

The next day the administrator, Warden Price, fearing further violence from the mob, swore in several special constables and five police constables were later sent to the area from Hokitika who ensured there was no more trouble.

Two of the ringleaders of the riot, William Quinlan and William Ryan, were arrested on charges of wilful damage, but the case against them was dropped because of a legal technicality.

By early April 1866 most miners had left the area, creating a problem for the Bruce Bay storekeepers who were left seriously out of pocket by the whole hoax. They were faced with endeavouring to sell their stock for whatever they could get for it, or with the significant cost of shipping it all back to Ōkārito.

They had large amounts of money invested in the stock in their stores, but fewer and fewer customers left to sell to. Signs appeared outside the stores advising: 'Selling Off Cheap', and they meant it. Prices were dropped sharply, in one case beef was selling for ninepence (8 cents) a pound, a fraction of the usual price.

As a further safeguard against any further hoaxes, Warden Price refused to grant any new prospecting claims in the area without first prospecting the ground himself or sending a constable to report on the site.

But there were some successes in the area. There were several successful claims on nearby beaches and inland from Ōkārito with some 12,000 ounces (340 kilos) of gold reportedly recovered.

By the end of 1866 virtually everyone had left, and the townships of Weld, Ōkārito, Five Mile Beach and Gillespies were abandoned.

It is believed Hunt left the coast by ship after avoiding the irate miners and was next heard of in Invercargill at the end of April. In mid-May he turned up at Riverton Aparima and then later at the Pahia diggings west of the town, along with a party of supporters. He told a local newspaper reporter that he believed as soon as the Pahia diggings were declared a goldfield, many leases would be taken up and large quantities of gold recovered.

However, the diggings never amounted to much, although mining did continue at Round Hill near Colic Bay until the 1950s, and there were minor gold finds at several other Southland sites, including Waimumu, Waikaia and Nokomai.

Hunt apparently engineered another hoax while he was in Riverton, encouraging a group of prospectors to head for Bruce Bay again. The hopeful miners arrived at Paringa in South Westland in July 1866, once again waiting for Hunt to join them, but he never arrived.

The group prospected the area while they waited, eventually giving up and trekking north to Ōkārito.

History doesn't record what happened to Hunt, who vanished after his Riverton appearance.

In the vernacular of nineteenth-century goldmining, a duffer rush, or duffer's rush, was a gold rush in which no gold is found.

# 1897

# RELIGIOUS SHYSTER, FALSE PROPHET AND CON ARTIST

Religious shysters are not just a phenomenon of modern times but have been a fact of New Zealand life since the early days.

One of the most notorious was an American known as the Rev. Arthur Bentley Worthington, whose real name was Oakley Crawford. He arrived in Christchurch in January 1890 and quickly established himself as leader of a cult that caused shock and dismay among the locals.

Crawford was born at Saugerties, Ulster County, in New York State on 1 March 1847, to Samuel Crawford (a lawyer) and his wife Susan (a schoolteacher). He was their third child and second son. He studied law at Columbia University but in January 1864 deferred his studies to enlist in the US Army during the American Civil War. He was assigned to the 5th Regiment, New York Heavy Artillery. He was serving with that Regiment when the war ended with victory to the North on 9 April 1865.

He returned to Columbia to complete his studies, graduating in 1867, and became involved with the Methodist Church. He married Josephine

*Notorious confidence trickster Oakley Crawford, aka Rev. Arthur Worthington. He was said to be 'tall and handsome with expressive steel-blue greyish eyes and an easy speaker'.*

W.A. Taylor Collection, Canterbury Museum

Moore in New York City on 23 May 1868, the first of his ten 'marriages' and the only legitimate one. Shortly after he embarked on his criminal career.

By all accounts, Crawford/Worthington was an impressive figure. He was described as tall and handsome with expressive steel-blue greyish eyes and fair hair. He was well spoken and an easy speaker.

His first brush with the law came in New York in 1870 when he was convicted of obtaining money by false pretences and jailed for three years. After his release he went through a series of identities and bigamous marriages and fraudulent relationships with at least eight wealthy women in many parts of America, apparently also fathering three children. In each case he moved on after he had swindled the women out of their money.

By 1889, he had become a faith-healer with the Church of Christ Scientist, a lay church with no organised clergy or religious ritual, founded in New England by Mary Baker Eddy in 1879.

He began an affair with Mary Plunkett, a married woman and editor of the church's international journal. The pair declared themselves to be soulmates and went through a sham wedding ceremony, which led to Plunkett's husband launching an inquiry into Worthington's background. That revealed that he was a serial conman with a string of female victims.

Worthington and Mary Plunkett, along with her two children, then fled to New Zealand, arriving in Christchurch in January 1890, where they quickly established their 'Students of Truth' sect, a revivalist Christian cult. In the city they found a ready source of converts willing to provide them with a generous cash flow.

Within two years the pair had built an extravagant headquarters for their cult alongside Latimer Square, and next to that, a magnificent twelve-roomed mansion for the couple and the children. The Temple of Truth building was opened on 11 August 1892.

It was built of wood in classic style, stood about three storeys high, and featured six Ionic columns supporting a simple pediment, with five small gables along one side, each with a round window. The other side was attached to their mansion.

Later it became a choral hall and then it was the Latimer community hall and dance hall until it was finally demolished in 1966 to make way for a new YWCA hostel that was never built.

*The Temple of Truth, Latimer Square, Christchurch.*
Ref: 1/2-020058-F, Alexander Turnbull Library, Wellington, New Zealand

It wasn't long, however, before rumours started circulating in Christchurch about Worthington's affairs with some of his women parishioners, his unorthodox doctrines and his teachings on free love and wife-swapping, which some said also included demonstrations given by the pair in private appointments.

The rumours and his unorthodox doctrinal teachings aroused the ire of established church leaders and one of them, the Rev. John Hosking of the St Asaph Free Methodist Church, began to inquire into Worthington's background, unearthing a sad tale of deception and fraud. Credit must be given to the *Christchurch Star* newspaper which latched onto Worthington's fraud in 1893 and campaigned against him.

Worthington denied all the allegations against him and continued to garner support from Christchurch's gullible and innocent, who stuck with him despite the mounting crescendo of criticism.

Amid this firestorm, he decided to get rid of Mary Plunkett after her money ran out. He expelled her from the church and from the family home and exiled her to Sydney, apparently with generous compensation. But Plunkett had herself built up a strong following within the church, with a clique known as the Order of the Temple. Rumour had it that this sect within a sect was even more extreme in its views of sex and in which promiscuity was rife.

Plunkett didn't go quietly, however, and was outspoken in her criticism of Worthington's morality and theology. That eventually led to a police investigation and an inquiry by the government, and unsuccessful attempts to persuade the United States to extradite him to answer for his earlier crimes in America.

Now the whole charade began to unravel, and this was compounded in August 1895 when he entered into a sham marriage with local woman Evelyn Maude Jordan, with whom he subsequently had four children.

In January that same year Worthington had entered into a contract with the trustees of the cult to purchase the Temple of Truth building and that debt, along with demands from others for him to pay back money he had borrowed from them, led to him and Evelyn fleeing New Zealand in December 1895. He told his remaining followers that he was going to the USA to collect funds owing to him, but it soon became apparent to the trustees that he had settled in Tasmania and that he had no intention of returning.

But astonishingly, when his Australian endeavours turned to dust after similar deceit and deceptions, he and Jordan did return to Christchurch on 9 September 1897, where he made plain his intention to re-establish himself and his cult, advertising a series of lectures at the Oddfellow's Hall in Lichfield Street, after the Temple of Truth refused to allow him to hold his meetings there.

He held four meetings in the hall, the first on Sunday, 12 September and a second on the following Sunday, both of which attracted large, hostile crowds.

At the 12 September meeting, at which he was to deliver a lecture on his work in Hobart and Christchurch and explain why he was returning to the city, hundreds were unable to get into the hall because of the numbers. The meeting broke up in disarray shortly after getting under way at 7 p.m., and Worthington had to be escorted by six policemen through a crowd that had gathered outside the hall who booed and yelled abuse at him. The police provided an escort to get him to his home, and they were followed on that journey by 'a mob of hooting boys'.

At his next meeting on 19 September there was more trouble. As Worthington left the hall after the lecture with several policemen at his side, he was again greeted by a hostile crowd of about a thousand who hooted and shouted abuse. Despite the efforts of a contingent of some 20 police, Worthington and his two assistants were 'very badly hustled' by the protestors. Police managed to hold off the crowd and escort Worthington and his helpers into Manchester Street and then north to Worcester Street East where they took shelter in the residence of a Mr A. Joyce, all the time followed and heckled by the crowd, many of whom belted him with sticks.

Once Worthington and his two supporters were safely inside the house, the crowd — which included quite a few women — continued to yell threats and abuse, and a torrent of stones was thrown at the house. After about an hour, the crowd drifted away.

Next day, Worthington appealed to the police and the Christchurch City Council for protection, but the Council turned him down, stating it had no authority to intervene, other than to restrict numbers attending the meetings.

Worse violence came at his third meeting on Sunday, 26 September 1897. Pandemonium and rioting broke out after that meeting for which — fortunately — a large number of police had been organised to try to keep the peace.

As the start time for the meeting drew near, about 1000 people had gathered in front of the hall to protest at Worthington's activities, whereupon some 40 police — four of them on horseback — including reinforcements brought in from all Christchurch's suburban stations from as far away as Kaiapoi, marched onto the scene.

As Worthington's interrupted address ended, the crowd numbers outside swelled considerably until an estimated 6000 restless and unhappy citizens were milling around the front doors of the hall where the mounted police and those on foot drove them back, clearing a space in front of the hall.

When Worthington came out of the hall at about 8.15 p.m. he was met by a hostile and vocal crowd, and the officer in charge of the police contingent, Inspector Broham, warned him that police couldn't guarantee his safety from the crowd if he left the scene on foot. A horse-drawn coach was called for him which arrived about half an hour later. Worthington and some of his friends were able to make their way from the hall into the coach, but it was blocked from proceeding by the crowd, which was growing more hostile. Two constables were posted with the two leading horses to keep them under control.

The situation had reached a heated and threatening stalemate, with several arrests made. Two local stipendiary magistrates, Mr H.W. Bishop and Mr R. Beetham, were in attendance, and after considering their options, Beetham climbed up onto the coach and read the Riot Act to the crowd.

The Riot Act allowed local authorities to declare a public gathering unlawful and order the assembly to disperse or face punitive action. It was the first and only time the Act would be read in Christchurch.

The wording was:

*Our Sovereign Lady, the Queen, chargeth and commandeth all persons being assembled immediately to disperse and peaceably depart to their habitations or to their lawful business, upon the pain of being guilty of an offence on conviction of which they may be sentenced to imprisonment with hard labour for life. God Save the Queen.*

His reading was interrupted with hissing, boos and derision from the angry crowd.

Beetham then ordered the police to clear a path for the coach. The mounted police charged the crowd while those on foot drew their batons and also charged, at which point the crowd fell back and moved from Lichfield Street into High Street, clearing the street in front of the hall. But the situation was far from under control, and Inspector Broham recommended to Worthington that he return to the hall for his own safety, but he refused. A few minutes later at 9.15 p.m. while the police held the crowd at bay in High Street, the horse and coach suddenly turned around and fled the area at speed, turning into Colombo Street, with two constables, who had been attending to the horses, clinging to the box seat.

Worthington and his entourage were dropped off at a house in north Colombo Street, but a crowd of about 800 protestors had followed them and gathered outside the property. The police contingent was also promptly on the scene and kept things under control until shortly after ten o'clock when the protestors drifted away and the police were able to return to the station.

Worthington held a fourth meeting on Sunday, 3 October, and this time a crowd of about 4000 gathered outside the hall, along with a large contingent of police, the Christchurch Mayor, Mr W.H. Cooper, and the two Stipendiary Magistrates, Beetham and Bishop. Threats of confrontation faded, however, when the fire alarm sounded, and the Fire Brigades turned up at the hall. There was no fire, and after checking the building, the brigades returned to their stations.

It was felt by the mob that perhaps Worthington had been whisked away by the departing Brigades, but in fact he had escaped through a back door and a right-of-way behind the hall and fled while the crowd was distracted by the arrival of the fire brigades.

The mob dispersed shortly after, and this time there were no arrests or violence.

There were rumours in Christchurch that authorities had arranged the false alarm so Worthington could escape the scene unharmed, but that suggestion was firmly rejected by the City Council, the police and the fire brigades.

Worthington remained in Christchurch for another two years after the riots but seems to have maintained a relatively low profile. He is believed to have finally left New Zealand in May of 1899, settling in Melbourne where he was soon up to his old confidence tricks again. He was arrested there in 1902 on charges of defrauding an elderly French widow and was sent to jail for seven years. On his release in 1909 he returned to the United States where he became a Presbyterian Minister at Poughkeepsie in New York State but was expelled from the Church soon after for preying on his congregation.

He kept up his swindling ways, however, and in July 1916 — under the name of Charles Graham Bone — he 'married' his tenth or eleventh wife, Mrs Jennie A. Showalter of Wilmington, Delaware. But that only lasted a few months before he deserted her, taking with him her life savings of $2500.

He was finally arrested by US authorities in January 1917 on multiple charges and remained in Newburg Prison in Orange County, New York, until his death on 13 December 1918, at the age of 69. It is said that he had a heart attack upon being confronted by one of his female victims.

His Christchurch 'wife', by this time known as Evelyn M. Crawford, claimed his military pension from his service in the Civil War. His body was interred at Poughkeepsie Rural Cemetery in Dutchess County, New York.

In 1961, the New Zealand Riot Act was incorporated into the Crimes Act, and in 1987 the requirement to 'read The Riot Act' was removed by the Crimes Amendment Act.

# SOURCES OF INFORMATION

Identifying the stories for this book came exclusively from my own *Today in History New Zealand* resource.

But that resource only highlights the brief facts of the stories and does not contain all the details, so filling out all the necessary facts and background about each has involved a huge number of sources, the great majority located online through the power of Google.

By far the greatest source of information has been the National Library's superb online Papers Past resource, an extraordinary collection of facts and information from our past that is a real taonga.

Other sources have included:

**Digital:**
Alchetron, The Free Social Encyclopedia
Alexander Turnbull Library
Auckland Art Gallery
Auckland Public Library
Canterbury Museum
Christchurch City Libraries
Invercargill Museum
JSTOR Digital Library

Jay McIntyre, JEM Aviation, Marlborough

Marlborough Aero Club, Omaka, Blenheim

Victoria University of Wellington's NZETC — New Zealand Electronic
    Text Collection

The Hocken Library

Museum of New Zealand Te Papa Tongarewa

National Library of New Zealand

New Zealand Legal Information Institute

RNZAF Museum — Wigram, Christchurch

Rootsweb

Tauranga Heritage Collection

Tauranga Historical Society

The Encyclopedia of New Zealand (Te Ara)

The New Zealand Journal of History, Department of History, University
    of Auckland

Toitū Otago Settlers Museum, Dunedin

University of Waikato

Wellington City Libraries

West Coast NZ History

Wikipedia

**Books:**

*Famous New Zealand Firsts and Related Record* (Alan Sutherland
    F.R.N.S., 1961)

*Hakoro Ki Te Iwi — The Story of Captain Howell* (Eva Wilson, 1975)

*Two Hundred Years of New Zealand History 1769–1969* (A.W. Reed,
    1979)

**Other:**

The author's own collection of historic facts:
*Today in History New Zealand*

Snippets of information have been obtained from a large number of
research papers, reports and thesis documents to be found online.

# INDEX

Page numbers in **bold** refer to images.